CONFESSIONS OF A
TRADITIONAL CATHOLIC

MATTHEW ARNOLD

CONFESSIONS OF A TRADITIONAL CATHOLIC

IGNATIUS PRESS   SAN FRANCISCO

Cover design by Davin Carlson

© 2017 by Ignatius Press, San Francisco
All rights reserved
ISBN 978-1-62164-155-1
Library of Congress Control Number 2017945960
Printed in the United States of America ∞

To Blessed Mary of Good Success:
Star of the Sea and loving helper
of the Christian people

Many of those who are humiliated
are not humble.
Some react to humiliation with anger,
others with patience, and others
with freedom.
The first are culpable, the next harmless,
the last just.

—Saint Bernard of Clairvaux

CONTENTS

FOREWORD

My friendship with Matthew Arnold arose, as friendships do, from many shared experiences. We both discovered the Catholic faith in adulthood—and fell in love with it. We both were drawn to tradition. We both determined, very soon after conversion, to dedicate our work, full-time, to the apostolate.

In fact, soon after meeting, we began working together. We broadcast many hours of live radio together. We spoke together at conferences. In all our collaboration we tried to communicate the beauty of tradition to an audience, mostly Catholic, who knew little or nothing about their own heritage. They couldn't number the Sacraments or name the commandments. They were strangers to the great saints, from Ignatius of Antioch and Augustine to Thomas Aquinas and Alphonsus Liguori. They were unaware of their obligation to attend Mass on Sundays and Holy Days of Obligation. If they thought about fasting at all, they viewed it as something done by Muslims and Jews, but not Catholics.

So with Matthew Arnold I shared a deep sorrow that so many people—whole generations within the Church—had been deprived of the riches of Catholic tradition. Through the last half century even the clergy experienced a disconnect, a rupture, a break with the past.

Such sorrow can lead to disaffection, if we let it. And not a few tradition-minded Catholics have let it—and let themselves lose their ardor for the faith, the Church, and the apostolate.

Not so Matthew Arnold. He sensed the danger, and he knew where one should always turn in danger. He went to the Blessed Virgin Mary, who led him to a greater understanding and love for all her children in the Church. He came to see that tradition and development are not opposed principles. He came to know that it's not either-or—it's both-and.

That, in fact, is the truly and traditionally Catholic approach.

This book is Matthew Arnold's story. It's not an argument. It's the beautiful story of how he found, and then lost, and then rediscovered the joy of Catholic tradition. It's the page-turning tale of how he stumbled again upon the peace that surpasses all understanding, even the clear understanding of our historical situation, which is admittedly dire.

This book is a much-needed expression of hope for our time—hope with its eyes wide open.

Scott Hahn, PhD
Steubenville, 2016

INTRODUCTION

No matter how "normal" a Catholic you are, I suspect you have heard about Catholic Traditionalism. Maybe you have friends or family that assist at the Extraordinary Form of the Mass, also known as the Traditional Latin Mass.[1] Maybe a church in your diocese offers this Mass at least sometimes. Maybe you've heard of the Society of Saint Pius X or other Traditionalist groups that operate outside the official structure of the Church and wondered what it was all about.

Let me say at the outset that my journey into the world of Traditionalist Catholicism was not motivated by any personal animus toward Vatican II or the "New Mass". As an adult convert, I had virtually no experience whatsoever of the "preconciliar" Church. A former New Age practitioner and Hollywood insider, I was only received into the Roman Catholic Church in 1996. Consequently, I had no nostalgia for the Latin language in general or the Traditional Mass in particular.

My Catholic formation was what many would call "solid and orthodox". By 1998 I was working

---

[1] The Extraordinary Form and the Traditional Latin Mass refer to Holy Mass celebrated in Latin according to the Roman Missal of 1962.

full-time in Catholic evangelization as an apologist, public speaker, and EWTN Radio personality. Pope Saint John Paul II was the first pope I ever knew, and the vernacular Mass, complete with lay lectors and guitar music (sometimes provided by me), was the liturgy that I embraced. I had no trouble back then reconciling the New Mass with the traditional doctrines of the Church, nor do I now.

So how did I wind up spending years at an "Independent" Traditionalist chapel outside the jurisdiction of the local bishop? Why did I eventually return to full communion with the Church? What did I learn on the way? I am writing this little book to provide the answers and, I hope, to promote greater understanding and unity within the Body of Christ.

Matthew Arnold
Garden Grove, 2017

Chapter One

In the Beginning

It all started with a question about the Eucharist. My wife, Betty, and I were married in the Church in 1991. I began attending Mass with her even before then, but never felt any particular urge to become Catholic. During our marriage preparation, I technically should have enrolled in the Rite of Christian Initiation of Adults (RCIA) but—presumably because I had no desire to convert—the priest who helped us through the process thought it better to delay my instruction. However, since part of the deal for getting married in the Church is to raise the children in the faith, he made me promise to take instruction "when the kids come along and start asking questions". Two years later, when we brought our first child, Macklin, home from the hospital, Betty immediately asked if I was going to enroll in RCIA. I replied, "It's not like he has questions. He can't even hold up his own head!" But it didn't take long.

I continued attending Mass with Betty and, now, little Macklin. When he was not quite three years old, Mack asked Mommy why everyone went to Communion except him and Daddy. Betty told him, "To receive Communion, you have to understand that the Host is Jesus." Macklin thought about this for a moment and then asked, "If that's Jesus, where is His hair?" Her response? "Go ask your father." Obviously caught flat-footed, I remarked that a certain priest at our parish, Father Magister,[1] seemed very sincere and, if he was the teacher, I would be willing to take the course. That was Sunday evening. On Monday morning Betty called the rectory to ask when RCIA classes began. Wouldn't you know it was that very Thursday? And who was the instructor? You guessed it.

DON'T TALK TO ME ABOUT IT

As my RCIA instructor, Father Magister was something of a perfect storm. A former Fundamentalist, he converted to Catholicism, answered the call to the priesthood, studied in Rome, and finally was ordained by Pope Saint John Paul II himself! It was a great blessing for me that Father wound up teaching RCIA at our little parish, Saint Ubiquitous.[2]

At the first class, we went around the room introducing ourselves and explaining why we were

[1] Real name withheld for prudential reasons.
[2] The real name of the parish has also been withheld for prudential reasons.

taking the course. The responses were what you might expect: "I'm Bob and I'm getting married in the Church"; "I'm Sue and I never got confirmed." When my turn came I said, "My name is Matthew and I have no intention of converting. I'm only here to find out what *you people* believe." I was never much of a "joiner".

Quite unexpectedly, I found Father's teaching style enormously appealing. For one thing, he was not shy about the "hard teachings" of the Gospel: that fornication and other sexual immorality is mortally sinful, that Christ forbade divorce and remarriage, that He only founded one Church, that receiving Communion unworthily is a sacrilege, and so on. In fact, he would boldly proclaim such teachings knowing full well he was making the Catholics in the room every bit as uncomfortable as the catechumens. Then, when the tension reached the level where you could cut it with a knife, he would shrug and say, "And if you don't like it, well, don't talk to *me* about it! Tell it to Jesus; it's His teaching." Father's insistence that he was simply handing on what he had received, along with his confident appeal to the authority of Christ and His Church, was a compelling combination. I admit I ate it up. Yet I still wasn't ready to convert.

I should mention that Father also did something that many today might consider rather radical. He had us begin each class by praying the Rosary together—on our knees—with the intention that the Holy Spirit would open our hearts and enlighten our minds. As I often say, I was praying the Rosary long before I became Catholic!

THE PENNY DROPS

Public prayer was something new for me. I was raised nominally Protestant, but "unchurched". Like millions of other families, mine had fallen away from attending Sunday services in the early sixties. We had a Christmas tree and Easter eggs like everybody else; we even retained the practice of grace before meals and prayers before bed, but I had no formal religious instruction and was never baptized. The fact is, growing up, the most Scripture I heard in a typical year was Linus reciting the Nativity story on *A Charlie Brown Christmas*.

Because of this, I survived more than one well-meaning attempt to get me "saved". In junior high an attractive young English teacher lured me into attending an after-school club meeting without mentioning that it was a Fundamentalist Bible study. That left a rather bad taste in my mouth, and I wondered what was wrong with Christianity that they had to try and trick you into it. A few years later, when a recently "born-again" friend offered me the customary invitation to ask Jesus into my heart, I inquired on what grounds I should accept Him as "my personal Lord and Savior".

"Because Jesus is the Son of God," was the ready answer.

"But *why* do you believe Jesus is the Son of God?" I asked.

"Because it says so in the Bible, which is the inspired word of God," he said.

"But *why* do you believe the Bible is the inspired word of God?" I pressed.

"Because it says so right here in Second Timothy: 'All scripture is given by inspiration of God, and is profitable for doctrine, for reproof, for correction, [and] for instruction in righteousness'."[3]

"Do you mean to tell me," I asked, "that you believe the Bible is inspired just because the Bible *says* it's inspired?" Even at seventeen I could see the critical flaw in such "Bible-based" religion. Consequently, I wrote Christianity off as just one more item on the spiritual smorgasbord. Like so many others of my generation, I drifted into various popular, but ultimately unsatisfying, New Age beliefs and practices that eventually left me a practical agnostic. But that's another story.[4] RCIA was different. About six weeks into the class we came to the apostolic succession:

> And I tell you, you are Peter, and on this rock I will build my Church, and the gates of Hades shall

[3] 2 Tim 3:16 (KJV).

[4] My conversion story, *Overcoming the New Age Movement*, is available on audio CD and MP3 download from Lighthouse Catholic Media at https://www.lighthousecatholicmedia.org/store/title/overcoming -the-new-age-movement.

not prevail against it. I will give you the keys of
the kingdom of heaven, and whatever you bind
on earth shall be bound in heaven, and whatever
you loose on earth shall be loosed in heaven. (Mt
16:18–19)

That's when the penny dropped. You see, the
handful of Evangelical and Fundamentalist Christians I had encountered exhibited a tendency to
look at the Bible like a man looking down a well.
All he can see is a long dark tunnel and his own
reflection at the other end. Likewise, my Bible
Christian friends seemed to project themselves onto
the New Testament and neglect everything that
happened between then and the Reformation.

Contemplating the apostolic succession, I got
a mental image of a line of popes stretching from
Pope Saint John Paul II all the way back to Saint
Peter. That's when I realized that the Catholic
Church is not "Bible-based"; rather, the *Bible* is
"Church-based" and the *Church* is "Christ-based".

The Catholic Church did not start with the Bible
and say, "Let's base a religion on this book!" Rather,
Christ founded the Church, and it was members
of the Church, the Apostles and their companions,
who wrote the documents that would become the
New Testament. Later, their successors, the Catholic bishops, met in council to determine the canon
(official table of contents) of the Bible. That's why
the Catholic Church has the right and duty to

interpret the Scriptures with authority, because she was there every step of the way. It's her book.

Founded by Jesus, the Catholic Church is the only Church that has existed from the first century until today—always led by a successor of Saint Peter. As the truth of this struck me, I knew I was in the right place. Suddenly I wanted to become Catholic more than I had ever wanted anything. I wanted a relationship with Christ and hungered to receive Him in Holy Communion. But I did not tell my wife just yet.

After the next class, as we were saying good night to Father, I simply asked what I had to do in order to get baptized. Betty's jaw dropped and she immediately started to cry. I tried to express my gratitude to Father, but he just said in his matter-of-fact way, "Don't thank me; it was the Holy Spirit." And then *I* began to cry.[5]

Betty's reaction came from the fact that she had prayed for years that, if I would open my heart the slightest crack, the Holy Spirit would come rushing in. As for me, coming to the realization that there is a personal God was a dramatic event in itself; discovering that He actually cares about *me* was quite frankly overwhelming. To this day I tell people that the apostolic succession was the intellectual lynchpin

[5] Before my conversion I could count the number of times I had cried on one hand. Now I cry all the time!

of my conversion. But that's not *why* I converted. I am Catholic today because of the free, unmerited gift of grace granted me by the Holy Spirit through the fervent prayers of my wife and the powerful intercession of the Blessed Virgin Mary.

At the 1996 Easter Vigil, to my great joy, I was received into the Body of Christ with the sacramental "grand slam" of Baptism, Confirmation, and First Holy Communion. It was genuinely life-changing. How much so, I would soon find out.

Entertainer to Evangelist

After a decade as a professional musician, I decided to switch media and pursue a living performing magic and comedy. In 1991 I became a full-fledged member of the world-famous Magic Castle and then a demonstrator at the legendary Hollywood Magic on Hollywood Boulevard. After my conversion, my magic career really started to take off. I worked as a "magic consultant" for network TV programs like *Weird Science*, *The Commish*, and *The Drew Carey Show*, among others. I also performed my magic for a dazzling array of 1990s A-list celebrities including Steve Martin, Danny Elfman, Rhea Perlman, and Quentin Tarantino, as well as iconic figures like Marlon Brando and Muhammad Ali. Speaking of iconic figures, the late pop superstar Michael Jackson once flew me from Los Angeles to New York just to spend an hour consulting with him about a certain magic trick. Two weeks later, when his recently estranged wife, Lisa Marie Presley, needed a magician for her thirtieth birthday party, I got the call.

Now I still had enough cultural Calvinism in me to assume that because I was materially successful, God must be really pleased with me—especially when my growing reputation led to a recurring gig as audience warm-up for the quintessential 1990s sitcom *Friends*, which, at the time, was the number-one show in the country. A "warm-up" is essentially an opening act that gets the audience laughing and builds up their enthusiasm before the show begins. In TV, this process continues throughout filming, keeping the studio audience happy and entertained during the frequent downtimes between takes. It was a great gig, and I was praying Rosaries of thanksgiving to and from Stage 24 at the Warner Brothers lot every week. But there was a hitch.

It took a while for me to realize that *something* just wasn't right. I worked on several morally questionable *Friends* episodes including *The One with the Lesbian Wedding* about Ross' (David Schwimmer) ex-wife marrying her same-sex partner, and *The One after the Super Bowl* featuring Julia Roberts as "Susie Underpants" and Jean-Claude Van Damme attempting to hook up with both Rachel (Jennifer Aniston) and Monica (Courtney Cox) at the same time.

But the problem finally became clear to me when we did *The One with the Chicken Pox*, which featured the May/September romance between Monica and Dr. Richard Burke, played by guest star Tom Selleck. As it turned out, Selleck and Courtney Cox were in bed together in all their scenes.

As usual, I stood in the audience between takes doing magic tricks, making jokes, and generally keeping everyone pumped up. At one point I shouted, "Isn't this great?" and they roared their approval. Just then a little voice inside my head said, "They're not married."

"Who's not?" I asked the little voice.

"Those characters. They're not married, but they're in bed together."

"And?"

"*And* that's a mortal sin. In fact, this whole show *revolves* around mortal sin. Do you know what that makes *you*? A *cheerleader* for mortal sin!"

The truth of this interior dialogue pierced my heart. So much so that I stopped accepting invitations to do warm-up on *Friends*.[6] And it was a costly decision.

From a worldly perspective it was crazy to turn down a gig with the number-one show on TV. It was glamorous, prestigious, and the pay was terrific. But, as my newly formed conscience pointed out, my responsibility as warm-up was, by definition, to

[6] Audience warm-up is typically contracted "show-to-show".

cheer on whatever was happening on stage—even if it was morally reprehensible. How could I go on encouraging people to laugh and applaud and, worse still, *approve* of mortally sinful behavior? To ask the question was to answer it. I decided to trust in God and the intercession of Mary and prayed that I would be able to find a job that would both support my family and bolster my faith. Thanks be to God, I did not have long to wait.

SAINT JOSEPH COMMUNICATIONS

During all these events, Betty and I volunteered for a local lay evangelization apostolate. It was there we met up-and-coming apologist Tim Staples. Shortly after I left *Friends*, Tim came to the house for a barbecue and announced he had taken a position as director of evangelization with Saint Joseph Communications (SJC). He revealed they were starting a radio ministry and encouraged me to approach SJC president Terry Barber about a position. I pitched myself to Terry, but, unfortunately, he decided they couldn't use me.

Then, out of the blue, Mark Wilson offered me a job with his company Magic International. Mark Wilson's work had been a huge influence on me. He was a star in the magic world and a pioneer of magic on television. Mark's company consulted for movies and TV (which is how he heard of me) as well as designing illusions for theme parks and

Broadway shows. They also had a retail arm. I was hired to handle that end and come up with new tricks for an upcoming TV infomercial to promote Mark's popular course in magic. It was a great opportunity, a chance to work with a boyhood hero, and best of all "family friendly". To say I was pleasantly surprised by this turn of events would be a gross understatement.

Three months later, Terry Barber called to say that SJC *could* use me after all. It felt like God was testing me. Leaving *Friends* had been a morally clear decision, however painful. But here was a choice between something good and, spiritually speaking, something better. Leaving Magic International meant another sacrifice—and would likely be the final nail in my showbiz coffin—but while the job with Mark *seemed* like an answer to my prayers, the position at SJC was something for which I had actually prayed.

Long story short, I soon found myself working full-time as the producer and announcer of three Catholic radio shows for SJC including *Reasons for Faith LIVE with Tim Staples* broadcast on the EWTN Global Catholic Radio Network.

A few months later I got a call asking if *I* would like to host a new program for EWTN Radio called *Scripture Matters LIVE with Dr. Scott Hahn*. After a couple of brief phone calls I found myself the producer of yet another worldwide Catholic radio broadcast, this time as the on-air host! Each week

I shared the mic with one of the most popular and influential Catholic theologians in the country. And I had barely been Catholic for two years!

Trouble in Paradise

In due time I was named creative director for SJC. I oversaw the production and marketing of all new audio and video products as well as the radio ministry. But the deeper I went into the Catholic lay apostolate, the greater my apprehension over the tension I found between the official teachings of the Church on the one hand, and my actual experience of Catholicism on the other. Answering the phones at SJC, I was routinely regaled with horror stories from Catholics around the country: from liturgical dancing to "Mass" celebrated with beer and pretzels to retreats where Catholics were encouraged to practice New Age "meditation"—basically emptying their minds and contemplating themselves instead of Christ. I was inundated with stories of the scandalous doctrinal and liturgical shenanigans of so-called liberal bishops, priests, and religious, not to mention Catholic educators. It was not long before it affected me personally.

Saint Ubiquitous had been a humble little parish when I took RCIA. But, like a potential convert who watches the Mass on EWTN and assumes it must represent a typical liturgy, I was in for a rude awakening. When our pastor retired and Father

Magister moved on to his next assignment, the coming of a new parish administration brought with it a tsunami of heterodox homilies, liturgical abuse, and open disdain for parishioners who simply wanted to live, believe, and worship like, well, Catholics.

Our new pastor had a penchant for inserting prayers of his own composition into the Ordinary of the Mass.[7] One of the most egregious was his "Invitation to Communion". Rather than offer the prescribed prayer at that time, "This is the Lamb of God who takes away the sins of the world. Happy are those who are called to His supper," Father would hold the Host above the Chalice and proclaim, "This is Jesus, who became a piece of bread for us." Keeping in mind that it is already a grave abuse to substitute his own prayer in the first place, his ad-libbed replacement was 180 degrees from the doctrine of Transubstantiation! As any Catholic second-grader knows, Jesus does not "become a piece of bread"! Rather, the bread substantially becomes the Body of Christ.

Another memorable episode was a homily by a certain new monsignor. The Gospel that Sunday was the Feeding of the Five Thousand.[8] In his homily, Monsignor explained that Jesus did not

---

[7] The Ordinary of the Mass consists of the texts of the Roman Missal that are generally invariable, in contrast with the "proper" prayers specific to the day or season.

[8] Jn 6:1–15.

miraculously multiply the loaves and fish. On the contrary, Monsignor said, everyone present carried food with them. But when the Apostles asked the crowd how much food they had, only one boy came forward with his five loaves and two fish.[9] So, Jesus said the blessing and began to distribute the five loaves, at which point, moved by Jesus' faith and shamed by the boy's example, everyone else contributed. Wonder of wonders, when they had finished eating, there was still some left over. So, according to Monsignor, the "miracle" was that Jesus got the Jews to share their lunch. I had heard of this sort of thing before, but was deeply scandalized when I experienced it personally.

Apart from the none-too-subtle racist subtext of this interpretation, it also expressly undermines Jesus' Eucharistic discourse that follows the next day. At the synagogue in Capernaum, Jesus tells the crowd, "Truly, truly, I say to you, you seek me, not because you saw signs, but because you ate your fill of the loaves."[10] Clearly the people were hoping that Jesus would repeat the miracle and feed them again. Instead, He used the opportunity to reveal *Himself* as the true Bread from heaven.[11] Which of course is the point of the miraculous multiplication in the first place.

---

[9] See Jn 6:9; cf. Mt 14:17; Lk 9:16.

[10] Jn 6:26.

[11] Cf. Jn 6:41.

Worst of all, Macklin was now old enough to be scandalized. "That's wrong, isn't it, Daddy?" he asked. "Jesus really multiplied the loaves and fish . . . didn't He?" I explained to Macklin that he had it right about the miracle and that Monsignor must be confused. Then I thought to myself, "Is this what I have to look forward to every Sunday?"

I later spoke privately with Monsignor and asked him the origin of his peculiar exegesis. He told me that he always had a "problem" with the miracle stories in the Bible, so when he encountered this "miracle of sharing" interpretation as a seminarian, he determined to share it at every opportunity in order to help others with similar issues. It seemed to me that Monsignor's real problem was unbelief and that heretical interpretations of Scripture were no cure. I asked if he also had a "problem" with the Resurrection. After all, Jesus raising Himself from the dead by His own power is somewhat more incredible than multiplying some bread and fish. After a prolonged moment of uncomfortable silence, Monsignor excused himself without answering.

I dubbed another of our new priests "Father Emcee" because he used his homily to "work the room" like a lounge singer. Wireless mic in hand, he would descend from the sanctuary. "Hi, where you from? Hey, that's my hometown!" Styling himself a biblical expert, he also insisted on introducing all the readings with "historical-critical" commentary that tended to undermine their content.

When I was lectoring one Sunday, Father said, "Matt's next reading was actually composed by an anonymous author around the middle of the second century." I then announced, "A reading from the Second Letter of Peter," which included the words:

We did not follow cleverly devised myths when we made known to you the power and coming of our Lord Jesus Christ, but we were eyewitnesses of his majesty. (2 Pet 1:16)

The problem is, what Scripture presents as an example of the eyewitness testimony of Saint Peter is somewhat less compelling if it was written a century after his death by someone else.[12]

On another Sunday, when I was lectoring, the Old Testament reading was the episode of Moses and the burning bush from the book of Exodus (3:1–12). This time, Father Emcee felt moved to comment on my "performance". He gushed, saying,

---

[12] Although there is general agreement that Second Peter was not written by Saint Peter, there are some in the Catholic Church who support the Petrine authorship. According to Catholic biblical scholars Scott Hahn and Curtis Mitch, "On balance, Peter's authorship has more in its favor than the modern theory of pseudepigraphical authorship." "Introduction to the Second Letter of Peter", in *The Letter of James, the First and Second Letters of Peter, and the Letter of Jude*, with Introduction, Commentary, and Notes by Scott Hahn and Curtis Mitch, and with Study Questions by Dennis Walters, Ignatius Catholic Study Bible, Revised Standard Version, Second Catholic Edition (San Francisco: Ignatius Press, 2008), p. 44; for a thorough explanation regarding the authorship of Second Peter, see pp. 43–44.

"I've been a priest for fifteen years and I've never heard that passage read so beautifully. C'mon folks, let's hear it for Matt!" Prolonged applause ensued. For me, this was just about the last straw.

You might think I was making too much of all this. But there was more behind my complaints than mere personal preferences. There is an old axiom, *lex orandi, lex credendi* (the law of prayer is the law of belief). In other words, there is a direct connection between liturgy and theology because *liturgy expresses doctrine*. Where there is poor liturgy, there is poor theology, and vice versa.

Take as a case in point a remark made by our pastor after Mass one Sunday. When we informed him that Betty was pregnant with our fourth child, he got an odd look on his face and told us, "I certainly hope you don't plan to have any more."

Somewhat taken aback, Betty said we would leave that up to God. But Father told us we needed to be "more responsible" and that "four kids is more than enough." The same fellow who claimed Jesus "becomes a piece of bread" was now telling us to close our marriage off from new life. *Lex orandi, lex credendi.*

Like millions of other Catholics, I could multiply such stories. Suffice it to say, the situation at Saint Ubiquitous had become intolerable, so we decided to look for a new parish. After all, there were three other Catholic churches within ten minutes of our house. Sadly, upon investigation, these communities proved no better. Everywhere we turned there were improvised prayers, insipid homilies, banal music, inappropriate applause, and armies of unnecessary lay "Eucharistic ministers".[13]

Speaking of inappropriate and unnecessary, during the homily at one church we visited, servers brought into the sanctuary a small table with a kitchen knife and some apples, while Father donned a chef's hat and apron over his vestments. He proceeded to play for laughs and applause while he lustily chopped up an apple, presumably to make some point about the day's Gospel. Unfortunately his message was totally lost on me due to my becoming physically ill over the idiotic impiety of the entire proceedings.

The above may sound harsh, but I use the word "idiotic" advisedly. Proverbs 9:10 says, "The fear of the LORD is the beginning of wisdom, and the knowledge of the Holy One is insight." The "fear" referenced here is the profound reverence due to God. It is not the servile fear of a slave for his master, but a filial fear, akin to the desire of a child to show due love, respect, and obedience in order to please

---

[13] Only the ordained are properly called Eucharistic ministers. When lay people distribute the Eucharist—Host or Chalice—they should be referred to as extraordinary ministers of Holy Communion. According to the General Instruction of the Roman Missal (GIRM), they are only to be employed when the size of the congregation, the incapacity of the celebrant, or the absence of any other proper minister (bishop, priest, or deacon) requires it (see GIRM 162).

a loving father. But that does not mean there are no consequences for abusing that relationship.

At the very least, liturgy that does not express profound reverence and recognition of the holy is neither wise nor prudent. On the contrary, I felt that priests and lay liturgists who introduced such irreverent nonsense were not just abusing the liturgy—which is bad enough—but also abusing their position, which really means abusing people. Parishioners cannot say Mass for themselves. They are dependent upon the parish to supply what the Church demands of a good Catholic.[14] And those in power *know it*.

When the parish does not fulfill its responsibility to provide a reverent liturgy, the parishioner who is offended by the unrelenting trivialization that the Eucharistic celebration is "the source and summit of the Christian life"[15] must continually confront the question, to whom shall I go?[16] I was now experiencing firsthand what Catholics from around the world had been complaining about for decades. At first I tried to follow the biblical prescription given by our Lord about when a "brother sins against

---

[14] The first precept of the Church obliges Catholics, under pain of sin, never to forego Mass on Sundays and Holy Days of Obligation through their own fault. See the *Catechism of the Catholic Church* (*CCC*), no. 2042.

[15] *CCC* 1324, quoting *LG* 11 [Vatican Council II, Dogmatic Constitution on the Church *Lumen Gentium* (November 21, 1964)].

[16] Cf. Jn 6:68.

you, go and tell him his fault, between you and him alone."[17] But personal corrections, appeals by groups of "two or three",[18] and finally "[taking] it to the church"[19] through complaints to the chancery all fell on deaf ears. I felt as if I was asking for bread, but was given a stone.[20]

AN OASIS IN THE DESERT

It was at this moment of feeling powerless and betrayed that someone suggested I attend a Traditional Latin Mass. I discovered that one was being celebrated locally under John Paul II's *Ecclesia Dei* indult.[21] Betty agreed to accompany me to this Indult Mass but left the kids with her sister. Having no experience with the Traditional Mass, she was concerned the kids might get fussy and disturb the other parishioners whom she assumed would be "old folks". As it turned out, the congregation was a mixture of people of all ages and ethnicities.

Several cities away from us, Saint Anonymous[22] was a little jewel box of a church largely preserved

[17] Mt 18:15.
[18] Mt 18:16.
[19] Mt 18:17.
[20] Cf. Mt 7:9.
[21] John Paul II's 1988 document *Ecclesia Dei* granted special permission for priests to publicly celebrate the Traditional Mass at parish churches with the permission of the local bishop.
[22] Real name withheld for prudential reasons.

from too much "liturgical renovation". Refreshingly Catholic as the building was—complete
with an altar rail—I found the rite itself sublime.
Here there was no applause, no banal music, no
improvised prayers or smarmy "wink-wink-nudge-
nudge" nonsense in the homily. Instead there was
reverence, beauty, dignity, and a tangible sense of
the sacred.

Assisting at my first Traditional Mass felt like a
crucial puzzle piece had finally fallen into place.
Here was what I had been looking for all along without even knowing it! I fervently prayed that Betty
would feel the same way. When Mass was over I
cautiously asked, "Well, what did you think?" Betty
looked at me and said, "I feel like I've just been to
Mass for the first time in my life."

Obviously, I do not mean to suggest that the New
Mass *cannot* be celebrated in a reverent way,[23] but
Betty and I both felt we had discovered "a pearl of
great price"[24] in the Traditional Latin Mass. Shortly
after our first experience at Saint Anonymous, we
became registered parishioners and started assisting
there regularly.

So what did we discover there that would move
my wife to abandon the parish in which she grew
up? After all, Betty's was one of the "founding

---

[23] I have already mentioned EWTN's televised Mass and my original experience with Mass at Saint Ubiquitous, for example.

[24] Cf. Mt 13:45–46.

families" of Saint Ubiquitous, and it was there that I was received into the Church. Before I answer that question, I think it well to describe briefly what I learned about the history of the Latin Rite from the Roman Missal of Pope Saint Pius V to the new Missal of Pope Blessed Paul VI.

CHAPTER TWO

A TALE OF TWO MISSALS

POPE SAINT PIUS V AND
THE TRIDENTINE MASS

Allowed by papal indult and with the permission of
the local bishop, the Mass celebrated at Saint Anon-
ymous followed the 1962 Missal of Pope Saint John
XXIII. This was the last revision of the traditional
Roman Missal before the promulgation of the new
Missal of Pope Blessed Paul VI in 1969.

Mass celebrated according to the 1962 Missal is
sometimes called the "Tridentine Mass" after the
Roman Missal of Pope Saint Pius V, promulgated
in 1570 at the request of the Council of Trent.[1] The
problem with the term "Tridentine Mass" is that
it implies that the traditional Missal was fabricated
by committee after the Council of Trent and then
imposed on the Church of those days from above.
On the contrary, in his 1570 decree *Quo Primum*

---

[1] The term "Tridentine" comes from *Tridentum*, which is Latin for
"Trent".

Pope Saint Pius V asserts that the Catholic Mass was returned to its original purity and relative simplicity. Rather than *reforming* the liturgy, he states, "Learned men of our selection ... have *restored* the Missal itself to the original form and rite of the holy Fathers."[2]

In his 2007 motu proprio[3] *Summorum Pontificum*, Pope Benedict XVI identified the organic development of the Tridentine Mass all the way back to the sixth-century reforms of Pope Saint Gregory the Great. In fact, there was nothing new in the Missal of Pius V. He merely codified the Roman Rite in response to the encroaching liturgical novelties of the Protestant Reformers. Put simply, the Church needed to be sure that what the faithful were getting was really Catholic.[4]

After *Quo Primum*, the liturgy remained substantially unchanged for centuries.[5] Nearly four hundred years later, one of the first documents to come out of the Second Vatican Council was *Sacrosanctum*

[2] Pius V, *Quo Primum* (July 14, 1570), no. 2, http://unavoce.org /resources/quo-primum/. All emphases in any quotations throughout are the author's unless otherwise noted.

[3] A document issued by the pope "on his own initiative" (Latin, *motu proprio*) and personally signed by him.

[4] To this end, liturgical rites more than two hundred years old (and therefore solidly pre-Reformation) were allowed by Pius V (see *Quo Primum*, no. 4).

[5] Some corrections and revisions to Pope Pius V's text were undertaken by Pope Clement VIII (1604), Pope Urban VIII (1634), and Pope Leo XIII (1884). However, these and subsequent Missals included the document *Quo Primum* to demonstrate the continuity among the various editions.

Concilium, the Constitution on the Sacred Liturgy. This document called for certain revisions of the Mass. The question is, why did the bishops at Vatican II believe it necessary to revise the Holy Mass at that precise moment in history?

Pope Saint Pius X—Liturgical Reformer

"Medievalism" was a nineteenth-century response to the dehumanization of the industrial revolution. The medievalists expressed themselves with architecture, literature, music, and art, as well as philosophy and theology. The Liturgical Movement began among the medievalists in an attempt to rediscover and renew the worship practices of the Middle Ages that were held as an ideal expression of the faith.

The Liturgical Movement for its part had a number of elements including scholarship, pastoral theology, and liturgical renewal. One of the movement's leading lights was Dom Prosper Guéranger. A French Benedictine, his research into the medieval period focused especially on recovering authentic Gregorian chant. He was also the author of a highly influential commentary, the multivolume opus *The Liturgical Year*.

The nineteenth century also saw important archaeological discoveries like the *Didache* (*Teaching of the Twelve Apostles*) and *The Apostolic Tradition of Hippolytus of Rome*. *The Apostolic Tradition* became particularly influential inasmuch as it contained the outline of a third-century liturgy. The Liturgical

Movement gained further impetus under Pope Saint Pius X.

For centuries the Church did not lay down set rules about how to pray at Mass. While some followed the actual prayers of the Mass,[6] the laity also commonly assisted "in spirit"—for example, according to the actions of the various parts of the Mass, reading appropriate prayers from a prayer book, reciting the Rosary, or practicing another private devotion during the liturgy.

Although these practices would continue well into the twentieth century, Pope Saint Pius X was already insisting, "One mustn't sing or pray *during* Mass, one must *sing and pray the Mass*."[7] From his pontificate onward, the faithful were encouraged to follow the Mass prayers word-for-word with a hand Missal, praying or singing aloud where appropriate.

An enthusiastic supporter of the Liturgical Movement, the pontiff issued a motu proprio on church music in 1903, inviting the laity to "active participation in the most holy mysteries and in the public and solemn prayer of the Church",[8] a term that was

[6] The Ordinary of the Mass, with the Latin and the vernacular in parallel columns, along with the Sunday Gospels and Epistles were available in many popular prayer books.

[7] Edgar Tinel, "Pie X et la musique sacrée", *Musica Sacra* 28 (1908–1909), quoted in Fr. Pascal Thuillier, "Saint Pius X: Reformer of the Liturgy", Angelus Online (September 2003), http://www.angeluson line.org/index.php?section=articles&subsection=show_article&article _id=2229.

[8] Pius X, *Tra le Sollecitudini* (November 22, 1903), https://adoremus .org/1903/11/22/tra-le-sollecitudini/.

a watchword for the Liturgical Movement. Some Traditionalists today downplay the radical nature of this document, insisting it is only about music. But the fact is, Pius X's encouragement of "active participation" was not just about the faithful singing hymns along with the choir, but for them to sing the Gregorian chant that includes the responses and common prayers: the Creed, the Gloria, the Sanctus, and so on—in other words, all the parts sung or recited by today's laity in the New Mass.

A quarter of a century later (and three decades *before* Vatican II), his successor Pope Pius XI declared:

> It is most important that when the faithful assist at the sacred ceremonies, ... they should not be merely detached and silent spectators, but, filled with a deep sense of the beauty of the Liturgy, they should sing alternately with the clergy or the choir, as it is prescribed.[9]

Thus, the responses were no longer to be the sole province of the altar servers. Quoting *Sacrosanctum Concilium*, Pope Blessed Paul VI would likewise reiterate that the faithful "should be able to sing together, *in Latin*, at least the parts of the Ordinary of the Mass" (no. 19).[10]

---

[9] Pius XI, *Divini Cultus* (December 20, 1928), https://adoremus.org/1928/12/20/on-divine-worship/.

[10] Paul VI, "Changes in Mass for Greater Apostolate" (Address to a General Audience, November 26, 1969), no. 13, taken from *L'Osservatore Romano*, Weekly Edition in English, December 4, 1969, https://www.ewtn.com/library/PAPALDOC/P6691126.HTM.

Pope Saint Pius X also introduced an entirely new arrangement of the Psalter for use in the Divine Office, also known as the Liturgy of the Hours. Along with the Mass, the Divine Office composes the Church's official daily liturgy. The sainted pope described his reform of the Office as "the first step to the *emendation* of the Roman breviary[11] *and the missal*".[12]

Not surprisingly then, Pope Saint Pius X later undertook a revision of the Roman Missal, although he did not live to see it published. This Missal was issued and declared the new Typical Edition[13] by his successor Pope Benedict XV in 1920. Pope Saint Pius X's revision actually made few changes to the prayers, but major changes were made to the rubrics,[14] changes that were ultimately not incorporated in the general rubrics, but printed in a supplementary section: *Additions and Changes to the Rubrics of the Missal.*[15]

SOME ASSEMBLY REQUIRED

Perhaps Pope Saint Pius X's most striking actions concerned the Holy Eucharist. He was the pope

---

[11] The book containing the texts for the Divine Office.

[12] Pius X, apostolic constitution *Divino Afflatu* (November 1, 1911), http://sanctaliturgia.blogspot.com/2005/11/divino-afflatu-english.html.

[13] The "Typical Edition" refers to the Latin text to which all subsequent printings must conform.

[14] Rubrics (Latin, *rubrica*, "red") are directions for the actions to be performed by the ministers during the liturgy. They are printed in red ink to distinguish them from the prayers to be recited.

[15] *Additiones et variationes in rubricis Missalis.*

who lowered the age for First Communion from twelve to the "age of reason", typically seven years old. Even more controversial was his call for frequent, *even daily*, Communion for the faithful.

Over the years, various factors had conspired to discourage lay people from receiving Holy Communion regularly. So much so that *The Catechism of the Council of Trent* declared:

> The faithful are frequently to be reminded that they are all bound to receive the Holy Eucharist. Furthermore, the Church has decreed that whoever neglects to approach Holy Communion once a year, at Easter, is liable to sentence of excommunication.[16]

To "receive the sacrament of the Eucharist at least during the Easter season" is number three on the list of precepts of the Church.[17] But in 1905, Saint Pius X published a decree that declared: "[It is] the desire of Jesus Christ and of the Church that *all of the faithful* should *daily* approach the sacred banquet."[18]

At the time, Pope Saint Pius X's exhortations were considered quite radical by some clergy and

[16] *Catechism of the Council of Trent* (Rockford, IL: TAN Books, 1982), 251.

[17] *CCC* 2042.

[18] Pius X, *Sacra Tridentina Synodus: De quotidiana SS. Eucharistiae sumptione* (December 20, 1905), https://www.ewtn.com/library/CURIA/CDWFREQ.HTM.

were not always met with docility. But it must be remembered that, serious as it may be, changes in the liturgy are not a matter of doctrine, but ecclesiastical law. *And the pope is the supreme legislator.*

In 1909, after getting the ball rolling on liturgical reform, Pope Saint Pius X called the National Congress on Catholic Works (*Congrès National des Oeuvres Catholiques*) in Belgium. Among the many influential points put forth at that conference were the following:

- *Liturgy* should be the means of instructing the people in faith and life.
- The Mass should be *translated into the vernacular* to further promote "active participation of the faithful".
- Worship should be understood as "the common action of the people of God" and *not something celebrated solely by the priest.*[19]

In the years between the world wars, a number of books were published promoting these ideas, collectively referred to as "assembly theology".

POPE PIUS XII

The heady atmosphere in the Liturgical Movement that followed Pope Saint Pius X's reforms led to the

[19] *Wikipedia*, s.v. "Liturgical Movement", last modified June 23, 2017, https://en.wikipedia.org/wiki/Liturgical_Movement.

multiplication of "experimental liturgies" promoting many of the liturgical practices that are common today. However, such unapproved experimentation ultimately raised concerns in Rome. In 1947, Pope Pius XII issued an encyclical, *Mediator Dei*, which praised efforts to encourage the participation of the faithful, but also warned of false innovations, radical changes, and Protestant influences on the liturgy. In regard to the good fruits of the Liturgical Movement, Pius XII wrote:

> They are to be praised who, with the idea of getting the Christian people to take part more easily and more fruitfully in the Mass, strive to make them familiar with the "Roman Missal," so that the faithful, united with the priest, may pray together in the very words and sentiments of the Church. They also are to be commended who strive to make the liturgy even in an external way a sacred act in which all who are present may share. This can be done in more than one way, when, for instance, the whole congregation, in accordance with the rules of the liturgy, either answer the priest in an orderly and fitting manner, or sing hymns suitable to the different parts of the Mass, or do both, or finally in high Masses when they answer the prayers of the minister of Jesus Christ and also sing the liturgical chant.[20]

[20] Pius XII, encyclical *Mediator Dei* (November 20, 1947), no. 105, http://w2.vatican.va/content/pius-xii/en/encyclicals/documents/hf _p-xii_enc_20111947_mediator-dei.html.

However, he also observed that it was a false opinion to "make so much of these accidentals as to presume to assert that without them the Mass cannot fulfill its appointed end".[21] Elsewhere in *Mediator Dei*, Pope Pius XII praised the Tridentine Mass of Pope Saint Pius V. However, he also claimed that, due to the insufficient resources available at the time, the sainted pontiff had failed to restore the liturgy truly to "the original form and rite of the holy Fathers" as asserted in *Quo Primum*. For instance, the General Intercessions ("Prayer of the Faithful") had not been restored.[22]

In 1955, Pope Pius XII radically reformed the liturgy of Holy Week and Pentecost Sunday, even allowing the vernacular for the renewal of baptismal promises.[23] Compared to the changes of Saint Pius X, this was a bold action—one that necessitated changes to canon law. Prior to Pius XII's restoration of the Easter Vigil, the 1917 Code of Canon Law required that Mass should not begin more than one hour before dawn or later than one hour after midday (excepting Midnight Mass at Christmas).[24]

[21] Ibid., no. 107.

[22] A remnant of the General Intercessions remains in the Traditional Mass. After the Creed, there is an invitation to prayer, but the celebrant then proceeds directly to the Offertory verse.

[23] Sacred Congregation of Rites, *Maxima Redemptionis Nostrae Mysteria* (November 16, 1955). English translation: in AAS 47 (1955) 838–847, https://www.catholicculture.org/culture/library/view.cfm?recnum=11136.

[24] *Codex Iuris Canonici* (1917), can. 821 §§1–2.

The restoration of the Vigils also required that the laws of fasting before Communion be amended. Rather than observing the ancient fast from midnight, Pius XII allowed that one need only fast from food for three hours before receiving Holy Communion, and water for one hour.[25]

He further removed from the Vigil of Pentecost the long series of six Old Testament readings, along with their accompanying Tracts[26] and Collects,[27] and authorized new texts for Palm Sunday, Holy Thursday, Good Friday, and the Easter Vigil. In that same year he also further simplified the rubrics of the Mass.[28] However, he stopped short of issuing a revised Typical Edition. That honor would fall to his successor, Pope Saint John XXIII.

GOOD POPE JOHN AND THE 1962 MISSAL

Canonized a saint in April 2014 by Pope Francis, John XXIII was elevated to the Chair of Peter in 1958. Still remembered by many as *il bueno papa* (the

---

[25] Current regulations call for fasting from food and drink for one hour, with water and medicine excepted.

[26] In the Traditional Mass, the Tract consists of the verse or verses that replace the Alleluia on days of sorrow or penance (e.g., during Lent).

[27] The Collect is an oration that concludes the introductory rite of the Mass.

[28] Pope Pius XII, *Cum Hac Nostra Aetate* (March 23, 1955).

good pope), Pope Saint John XXIII was the first
pontiff of the twentieth century to make pastoral
visits in the Diocese of Rome, visiting prisoners,
inmates at a reform school, and patients in hospitals.
He dropped the use of the royal "we" on informal
occasions and became the first pope to travel outside of Rome since Pius IX.

In 1962, Pope John issued yet another new
Typical Edition of the Roman Missal incorporating a simplified Code of Rubrics prepared by the
commission of Pope Pius XII. The motu proprio
Rubricarum Instructum took the place of the apostolic
constitution *Divino Afflatu* of Pope Pius X. Among
these revisions, what garnered the most attention
was the removal of the adjective *perfidis*[29] in the
Good Friday Prayer for the Jews, and the insertion
of the name of Saint Joseph into the Roman Canon
(the Eucharistic Prayer).

Apart from the addition of prefaces and prayers
for new feast days, up to this time revisions of the
Roman Missal were usually considered more a
matter of *restoration* than *reformation*. Therefore, in
keeping with the preceding Typical Editions of
the previous four centuries, Saint Pius V's *Quo Primum* was included in the Missal of Pope Saint John
XXIII. Including *Quo Primum* served to demonstrate, despite the various revisions made over the

[29] "Faithless".

centuries, that this Missal was still substantially the Missal of Pope Saint Pius V. That was about to change.

SACROSANCTUM CONCILIUM

In 1959, Pope Saint John XXIII called the Second Vatican Council. In 1963, six months after Pope John's death, the Council Fathers, by an overwhelming majority, adopted *Sacrosanctum Concilium*, the Constitution on the Sacred Liturgy. Among the various proposals put forth in this historic document was a further revision of the Holy Mass so that the nature and purpose of the liturgy would be more clearly manifested. The rites were to be "simplified", and "elements which, with the passage of time, came to be duplicated" were to be discarded while others that had been lost due to the "accidents of history" were to be restored.[30] The Divine Office, or Liturgy of the Hours, would also be reformed along the same lines.

For the first time in the Latin Rite, the vernacular would be permitted for the readings and the prayers common to the people. Liturgies could even express local culture, subject to approval by the

---

[30] Vatican Council II, Constitution on the Sacred Liturgy *Sacrosanctum Concilium* (December 4, 1963), no. 50, http://www.vatican .va/archive/hist_councils/ii_vatican_council/documents/vat-ii_const _19631204_sacrosanctum-concilium_en.html. Hereafter cited as *SC*.

Holy See, yet the document reiterated that the faithful should be able to recite the Ordinary of the Mass *in Latin*.

POPE BLESSED PAUL VI

In 1964, Good Pope John's successor Pope Paul VI established the *Consilium ad exsequendam Constitutionem de Sacra Liturgia*, the Consilium for Implementing the Constitution on the Sacred Liturgy. The head of the Consilium was Monsignor Annibale Bugnini, who had been instrumental in the revision of Holy Week for Pius XII.

Between 1965 and 1969, the Consilium issued several instructions and permissions to be implemented during the interim between *Sacrosanctum Concilium* and the publication of a revised Typical Edition of the Roman Missal. These instructions and permissions included the following:

- even wider use of the vernacular
- allowing the priest to face the congregation (*ad populum*) instead of facing east (*ad orientum*)
- omission of the Psalm *Judica me*[31] at the foot of the altar
- suppression of the *Last Gospel* and the *Prayers after Low Mass*
- simplification of the rubrics and the vestments

[31] Ps 42:1 (DRV): "Judge me, O God ..."

- concelebration and distributing Communion under both kinds
- introduction of three new Eucharistic Prayers in addition to the Roman Canon

In 1969, Pope Paul VI promulgated his new Roman Missal with the apostolic constitution *Missale Romanum.*

And nothing has been the same since.

CHAPTER THREE

SAINT ANONYMOUS

It soon became common knowledge that my family and I were assisting at the Traditional Mass. I suspected that some folks would be curious about our decision, but I must admit I was surprised by the reaction of a retired Jesuit friend of mine: "Be careful," he said; "those people are crazy!"

"What do you mean, Father?" I asked.

"They don't have the mind of the Church!" he said. "Why, for all you know, you might be sharing the pew with a *sedevacantist*!"[1]

Well, I had a couple of objections to his line of thinking. Firstly, no self-respecting sedevacantist would attend *any* diocesan Mass, traditional or not,

[1] The name "sedevacantist" comes from term *sede vacante* (Latin for "the seat is empty"), which describes the interregnum between the death of one pope and the election of his successor. The sedevacantist position holds the documents of Vatican II, the New Mass, and other modern teachings to be heretical. Therefore, since one must be Catholic to be pope, sedevacantists reject the legitimacy of the recent popes on the grounds that they have all incurred automatic excommunication for heresy.

precisely because such celebrations *are in union with the pope* and pray for him by name in the Canon. However, my response to Father was rather more pointed: "With all due respect, I *may* share a pew with a sedevacantist at the Indult Mass, but at the *Novus Ordo*,[2] I know beyond a reasonable doubt I share a pew with people who engage in premarital sex, use artificial contraception, are "pro-choice", support same-sex unions, and still consider themselves 'good Catholics.'" Where, I wondered, was the greater danger of my fellow parishioners' heterodoxy "rubbing off" on me?

I felt secure in the fact that I was attending a diocesan Mass with the approval of the bishop. Law and order every time, that's me. I could not be responsible for what other people do or think. However, I must admit that the differences between the old and new Missals were beginning to affect my perspective on a number of issues.

At first glance, the main difference between the Traditional Latin Mass and the *Novus Ordo Missae* was the language. Instead of the vernacular, Latin was used throughout. The next most obvious difference was that the priest faced the altar instead of the people. But as I started to follow the Traditional Mass with a Missal, I discovered that the prayers and readings were also different. It may not surprise you to learn that these are some of the very points that

---

[2] *Novus Ordo Missae* is Latin for "New Order of the Mass".

gave rise to the Traditionalist Movement in the first place. This would lead to another turning point in my journey, when the bishop unexpectedly decided to terminate the celebration of the Indult Mass at Saint Anonymous. Perhaps my reaction to such a development is what my Jesuit friend was really worried about.

Lingua Angelica

While *Sacrosanctum Concilium* allowed for the readings and the proper prayers of the Mass to be said or sung in the vernacular, it also declared that Latin was to be retained in the liturgy and the faithful were expected to learn to sing and pray their parts of the Ordinary in Latin.

It is doubtful that the majority of Council Fathers would have signed *Sacrosanctum Concilium* if it had proposed celebrating the entire Mass in the vernacular, most especially the Roman Canon. However, there were so many instructions and permissions granted between 1965 and 1970 that by the time the *Novus Ordo* was promulgated, the celebrant was not obliged to say so much as a *single word* in Latin.

As a fledgling apologist, I had cut my teeth on standard books like *Faith of Our Fathers*[3] and *The Catholic Church Has the Answer*.[4] In these

[3] James Cardinal Gibbons, *Faith of Our Fathers* (Baltimore, 1876).

[4] Paul Whitcomb, *The Catholic Church Has the Answer* (Los Angeles: Loyola Book Company, 1961).

and other works—going all the way back to the Reformation—Catholic apologists defended the use of Latin against those who would object to celebrating the Mass in a "dead language".

Two thousand years ago, Latin was the universal language of the Roman Empire and quickly became the official language of the Catholic Church in the West. Even after Latin was no longer a spoken language, it remained the language of educated people well into the twentieth century.[5] For hundreds of years it was the boast of Catholics that they could assist at Mass anywhere in the world because the liturgy was the same everywhere. Also, unlike modern spoken languages, the meaning of Latin words does not change over time. Latin may be a "dead language", but it cannot become passé.

Ironically, Pope Saint John XXIII, best remembered for convening Vatican II, was adamant about the importance of Latin for clergy and laity alike. He wrote an encyclical on the subject that made these very points:

> Furthermore, the Church's language must be not only *universal* but also *immutable*. Modern languages are liable to change, and no single one of them is superior to the others in authority.[6]

---

[5] This is largely because many subjects were once learned mainly by reading primary sources.

[6] John XXIII, *Veterum Sapientia* (February 22, 1962), https://adoremus.org/2007/12/31/Veterum-Sapientia/.

He quoted Pope Pius XI to the effect that

> for the Church, precisely because it embraces all
> nations and is destined to endure to the end of time
> ... of its very nature requires a language which is
> universal, immutable, and non-vernacular.[7]

Saint John XXIII's successor, Pope Paul VI, for
his part admitted that the abandonment of Latin
gave Catholics "reason indeed for regret".[8] In his
address making the celebration of the New Order of
the Mass obligatory, he referred to it variously as a
"new rite",[9] an "innovation",[10] and even a "many-
sided inconvenience".[11] But he identified "the
greatest newness"[12] to be the change from Latin to
the vernacular. Realizing that this change would
upset many, Blessed Paul VI assured the faithful that
Latin would not vanish altogether. Referencing
Sacrosanctum Concilium, he said:

> But, in any case, the new rite of the Mass provides
> that the faithful "should be able to sing together,

[7] Pius XI, *Epist. Ap. Officiorum Omnium* (August 1, 1922), quoted
in *AAS* 14 (1922): 452.

[8] Paul VI, "Changes in Mass for Greater Apostolate" (Address to a
General Audience, November 26, 1969), no. 9, taken from *L'Osservatore Romano*, Weekly Edition in English, December 4, 1969, https://
www.ewtn.com/library/PAPALDOC/P6691126.HTM.

[9] Ibid., nos. 1–2, 13, 17–18.

[10] Ibid., nos. 1, 5.

[11] Ibid., no. 4.

[12] Ibid., no. 8.

in Latin, at least the parts of the Ordinary of the Mass" (*SC* 19).[13]

Still, Pope Paul was resolute in his decision to introduce the vernacular—regardless of the cost of abandoning Latin—for one reason in particular:

> What can we put in the place of that language of the angels? We are giving up something of priceless worth. But why? What is more precious than these loftiest of our Church's values? The answer will seem banal, prosaic. Yet it is a good answer, because it is human, because it is apostolic. Understanding of prayer is worth more than the silken garments in which it is royally dressed. Participation by the people is worth more—particularly participation by modern people, so fond of plain language which is easily understood and converted into everyday speech.[14]

But language was not the only thing to change.

Blessed Paul VI admitted that the new Missal was "a change in a venerable tradition that has gone on for centuries ... something that affects our hereditary religious patrimony, which seemed to enjoy the privilege of being untouchable and settled".[15] While he focused on the loss of Latin in particular, he also acknowledged:

[13] Ibid., no. 13.
[14] Ibid., nos. 9–11.
[15] Ibid, no. 2.

This change will affect the ceremonies of the Mass. We shall become aware, perhaps with some feeling of annoyance, that the ceremonies at the altar are *no longer being carried out with the same words and gestures* to which we were accustomed.[16]

But Pope Paul VI assured the faithful, saying,

Finally, if we look at the matter properly we shall see that the fundamental outline of the Mass is still the traditional one, not only theologically but also spiritually.[17]

The "fundamental outline" notwithstanding, some of the changes were the cause of more than mere "annoyance".[18]

[16] Ibid., no. 3.
[17] Ibid., no. 15.
[18] Ibid., nos. 3–4.

Chapter Four

If It Ain't Broke . . .

Attending the Indult Mass was a blessing, but it did not afford me peace of mind. On the contrary, it increased my agitation by raising more questions than it answered. I considered the Traditional Mass theologically rich and aesthetically beautiful to a degree unapproached by any celebration of the *Novus Ordo* I had ever witnessed. I kept thinking of an old saying my dad taught me as a child: "If it ain't broke, don't fix it."

I went back to Vatican II's Constitution on the Sacred Liturgy to find an answer for the rationale behind the more drastic innovations. According to *Sacrosanctum Concilium*:

> In the restoration and promotion of the sacred liturgy, this *full and active participation* by all the people is the aim to be considered *before all else.* . . . And, therefore, pastors of souls must zealously strive to *achieve it, by means of the necessary instruction*, in all their pastoral work.[1]

[1] *SC* 14.

In the words of the Council, then, pastors were to promote more active liturgical participation especially through instruction. This is consistent with the policy of the preceding century: teach the people to participate in the Mass. Nothing new here. When *Sacrosanctum Concilium* does mention making changes in the liturgy, it is with the following provisos:

> There must be *no innovations* unless the good of the Church genuinely and *certainly* requires them; and care must be taken that any new forms adopted should in some way *grow organically* from forms already existing.[2]

Nonetheless, it seemed clear to me that many of the changes authorized by the Missal of Paul VI were of dubious necessity and anything *but* organic.

DIS-ORIENTATION

Apart from language, one of the first differences I noticed at the Indult Mass was the priest facing the altar. Throughout history the priest and the people both faced *ad orientum*, "toward the east", which is considered symbolic of God generally and the Resurrection in particular. Facing east shows that the prayers of the priest are not addressed to the assembly, but to God. Nor is the Mass primarily a dialogue

[2] Ibid., 23.

between the priest and the people anyway, but a dialogue between God and His people in which the priest stands as mediator between the faithful and the altar. According to the future Benedict XVI:

> Josef Andreas Jungmann, one of the architects of the Council's Constitution on the Sacred Liturgy, was from the very beginning resolutely opposed to the polemical catchphrase that previously the priest celebrated "with his back to the people"; he emphasized that what was at issue was not the priest turning away from the people, but, on the contrary, his facing the same direction as the people.[3]

Cardinal Ratzinger insisted this was the constant Tradition of the Church. And technically, it still is. A careful examination of the rubrics for the Latin Typical Edition of the Missal of Paul VI reveals that the celebrant is instructed to "turn and face the people" at several points in the Mass (e.g., at the *Orate fratres*, "Pray brethren"). Now, unless he is expected to spin 360 degrees like a figure skater, then the new Missal actually assumes that the priest is facing the altar at the Offertory and the Eucharistic Prayer. This also is fitting:

> The Liturgy of the Word has the character of proclamation and dialogue, to which address and response can rightly belong. But in the Liturgy of

[3] Joseph Cardinal Ratzinger, foreword to *Turning towards the Lord: Orientation in Liturgical Prayer*, by U. M. Lang (San Francisco: Ignatius Press, 2004), 9.

the Eucharist the priest leads the people in prayer and is turned, together with the people, towards the Lord. For this reason, Jungmann argued, the common direction of priest and people is intrinsically fitting and proper to the liturgical action.[4]

The Mass is primarily a sacrifice, and sacrifice requires an altar. To facilitate Mass facing the people, the old high altars were replaced with freestanding altar tables. According to Cardinal Ratzinger, the "table form" altar and celebration *versus populum* (Latin, facing the people) "really does look like the characteristic fruit of Vatican II's liturgical renewal" but "brings with it a new idea of the *essence* of the liturgy—the liturgy as a communal meal".[5] This is in spite of the fact that

> nowhere in Christian antiquity, could have arisen the idea of having to "face the people" to preside at a meal.... The Lord established the new reality of Christian worship in the framework of a (Jewish) Passover meal, but it was precisely this new reality, *not the meal as such*, that he commanded us to repeat.[6]

The future Benedict XVI affirmed that even Jesus and the Apostles were on the *same side* of the table at the Last Supper. Further, "There is nothing in the Council text about turning altars towards the people; that point is raised only in post-conciliar

---

[4] Ibid., 11.

[5] Joseph Cardinal Ratzinger, *Spirit of the Liturgy* (San Francisco: Ignatius Press, 2000), 77.

[6] Ibid., 78.

instructions."[7] He insisted that celebrating the Liturgy of the Eucharist *versus populum* requires abandoning the ancient and constant practice of the Catholic Church and makes the *priest* the real point of reference for the whole liturgy:

> The turning of the priest toward the people has turned the community into a self-enclosed circle. In its outward form, it no longer opens out on what lies ahead and above, but is closed in on itself.[8]

This change was not organic, nor did it proceed from any tradition but the alleged practice of the ancient Church, even though Pius XII warned in *Mediator Dei*, "But it is neither wise nor laudable to reduce everything to antiquity by every possible device. Thus ... one would be straying from the straight path *were he to wish the altar restored to its primitive tableform*."[9] Yet, in March 1965—years before the promulgation of his new Missal—Paul VI celebrated his very first vernacular Mass on a table and facing the people.

CANON FODDER

The Missal of 1962 also revealed that the Roman Canon is the only "Eucharistic Prayer" of the

---

[7] Ratzinger, foreword to *Turning towards the Lord*, 9.

[8] Ratzinger, *Spirit of the Liturgy*, 80.

[9] Pius XII, encyclical *Mediator Dei* (November 20, 1947), no. 62, http://w2.vatican.va/content/pius-xii/en/encyclicals/documents/hf_p-xii_enc_20111947_mediator-dei.html.

IF IT AIN'T BROKE ...

Traditional Mass. The word "canon" means a "fixed rule" because this prayer was always the same, making "additional canons" something of an oxymoron. Still, between the end of Vatican II and the promulgation of the Missal of Paul VI, there were added to the Mass three *new* Eucharistic Prayers as alternatives to the Roman Canon, now commonly referred to as Eucharistic Prayer I.

In my experience of the *Novus Ordo*, the Roman Canon is rarely used, the much shorter Eucharistic Prayer II being the most common. Eucharistic Prayer II was taken from the so-called Canon of Hippolytus.[10] According to Father Joseph Fessio, S.J., a former student of Joseph Ratzinger (the future Pope Benedict XVI) and the founder of Ignatius Press, this prayer

> was probably never used as a liturgical text.... If it was, it ceased being used at least 1600 years ago. Yet from the [Second Vatican] Council, which says changes ought to come through organic growth and there should be no changes unless necessary, we come to liturgists saying, "Oh, let's pull this thing out of the third century and plug it back into the twentieth." That's not organic growth; that's archeologism,[11] specifically criticized by Pius XII in *Mediator Dei*.[12]

[10] Remember *The Apostolic Tradition of Hippolytus of Rome*?

[11] Aka "antiquarianism": preferring older forms simply because of their antiquity.

[12] Fr. Joseph Fessio, "The Mass of Vatican II", *Catholic Dossier*, September/October 2000, http://www.ignatiusinsight.com/features 2005/fessio_massv2_1_jan05.asp.

Well, at least Eucharistic Prayer II has a historical background. Eucharistic Prayer III was a pure invention. In the words of Father Fessio, "There has never been a canon like the Third Canon in the history of the Church, except in bits and pieces.... It's not organic; it's constructed."[13]

Eucharistic Prayer IV, based on an Egyptian canon, is seldom used today. Incompatible with the other prefaces, it has, for all intents and purposes, fallen by the wayside. "The point is," argues Father Fessio, "that the Council *did not* call for a multiplication of canons."[14]

AN OFFER YOU CAN'T REFUSE— OR CAN YOU?

The Offertory is the beginning of the "Mass of the Faithful" and the first principal part of the Traditional Mass.[15] This prayer is packed with doctrinal content, including sacrifice, the sinfulness and unworthiness of the priest who offers, purgatory, the distinction between the ordained priesthood and the common priesthood of the faithful, and the connection between this sacrifice and salvation.

---

[13] Ibid.

[14] Ibid.

[15] Traditionally, "the principle parts of the Mass" were those at which one must be present in order to fulfill his Sunday obligation: the Offertory, the Consecration, and the priest's Communion.

All of these beliefs were denied by the Protestant Reformers who naturally despised the Offertory. Martin Luther called it an "abomination" and asserted, "From this point almost everything stinks of oblation"[16] (i.e., sacrifice). It was removed from Protestant services precisely to demonstrate that, in their opinion, the Mass is *not* a sacrifice. The Offertory was likewise replaced in the *Novus Ordo* by the Prayer over the Gifts. Based on a Jewish grace before meals, the Prayer over the Gifts was also founded on the *Apostolic Tradition of Hippolytus of Rome.*

According to the lights of the Consilium, the old Offertory was wrong to refer to the bread as a "host" and a "victim" as there has not yet been a sacrifice, although such prayers are common to ancient Eastern liturgies as well. If this rationale is correct, it represents a condemnation of liturgical practice of both East and West for nearly sixteen centuries. What other reason could account for the change? According to the chief architect of the New Mass, Monsignor Annibale Bugnini, one of the Consilium's guiding stars regarding changes in the Missal was

the desire to help in any way the road to union of the separated brethren, by removing every stone

---

[16] F. A. Gasquet, *Edward VI and the Book of Common Prayer* (London: John Hodges, 1890), 221, quoted in Michael Davies, *Liturgical Time-bombs in Vatican II* (Rockford, IL: TAN, 2003), 318.

that could even remotely constitute an obstacle or difficulty.[17]

In the case of the Offertory, the dictate of *Sacrosanctum Concilium* that liturgical changes are only to be made in cases when "the good of the Church genuinely and certainly requires them" and "that any new forms adopted should in some way grow organically from forms already existing" did not seem to be a consideration.[18]

"TRI-CYCLE"

Sacrosanctum Concilium also called for liturgical Scripture readings to be "more varied",[19] and directed that the "treasures of the bible are to be opened up more lavishly."[20] Consequently, new Bible readings were added to the Missal. Many Catholics, myself included, consider the greatly increased proportion of biblical readings at Mass to be one of the genuine fruits of the liturgical renewal. Even before Pius XII suppressed the six Old Testament readings from the Vigil of Pentecost, only about 1 percent of the Old Testament (without Psalms) and 16.5 percent of

---

[17] Msgr. Annibale Bugnini, "The Variations of Some Texts of Holy Week", *L'Osservatore Romano*, March 19, 1965, 4, quoted in *Reasons for Resistance: The Hierarchy of the Catholic Church Speaks on the Post-Vatican II Crisis*, trans. Jason Roberts, O.S.S.M. (Jacksonville, FL: Queen of Martyrs Press), 21.

[18] *SC* 23.

[19] *SC* 35.

[20] *SC* 51.

the New Testament was read at Mass. In Paul VI's Missal, 13.5 percent of the Old Testament and 71.5 percent of the New Testament are read.[21]

The increase was accomplished by adding Old Testament readings to Sundays and major feast days, giving each weekday its own unique readings,[22] and replacing the ancient yearly cycle of readings with a new three-year cycle (A, B, and C) for Sundays and a new two-year cycle for weekdays. Considering the many prayers that are also based on biblical texts (e.g., Sanctus, Gloria, Angus Dei, Domini non sum dingus, etc.), it is the boast of the *Novus Ordo* liturgy that a Catholic who makes his Sunday obligation hears all the most important parts of the Bible proclaimed over the course of three years.

But concerns over assembly theology and active participation also overthrew two thousand years of Tradition and constant practice by inviting lay women into the sanctuary to help read it all.

HANNIBAL'S LECTORS

A proliferation of lay men and women in the sanctuary is commonplace today, but what are the implications? I recall a conversation in 1998 with a certain lady who was terribly upset with

[21] Fr. Felix Just, S.J., "Lectionary Statistics", Catholic Lectionary website, last updated January 2, 2009, http://catholic-resources.org /Lectionary/Statistics.htm.

[22] Sunday and feast day readings are sometimes repeated on weekdays in the Traditional calendar.

John Paul II's permission for the use of altar girls. Somewhat bemused, I asked her, "Are you a lector or an extraordinary minister?" "Both," she answered proudly. "Well then," I explained, "you lost this battle the day you stepped into the sanctuary. Really. What's more scandalous, little girls handling the vessels while assisting at the altar, or grown women handling the Body of Christ with unconsecrated hands?" Her response is unprintable but suffice it to say that not everyone has the same appreciation of irony. Point being: all the above is officially approved for the *Novus Ordo Missae*, but not the Traditional Mass.

New Prayers for Old

Adding the Old Testament readings led to another innovation—namely, the Responsorial Psalm.[23] The addition of this antiphonal prayer was accompanied by the suppression of the Gradual, which, also taken from the Psalms, is sung before the Gospel between the Epistle and the Alleluia in the Traditional Mass.

I remember sharing my take on this with one of my better-known colleagues by comparing classical opera to a campfire sing-along. While virtually *anyone* can recognize that singing opera requires genuine talent refined by years of training, it also requires attention and investment on the part of the listener in order to appreciate it truly. The campfire song,

---

[23] Invariably led by a lay lector or sung by a lay cantor.

by contrast, is intended to be so drop-dead simple as to enable anyone to sing along on a single hearing (e.g., "B-I-N-G-O, and Bingo was his Name-O!").

This, I concluded, was not unlike the difference between the settings for the Gradual and the Responsorial Psalm. The Gregorian chant settings of the former take training and dedication to sing well, and attention and investment is required for due appreciation—whereas the folk/pop melodies for the latter constitute a conscious reduction to the lowest common musical denominator so that everybody can "actively participate" without effort or preparation. When Saint Augustine said, "He who sings well prays twice," he was not talking about the congregation singing along with the choir.

Unfortunately, this concession to "active participation" meant abandoning some of the finest musical settings ever produced by Western culture. Once again, this was neither organic nor consistent with the Council's instruction that "other things being equal, [Gregorian chant] should be given pride of place in liturgical services."[24]

ACCENTUATE THE POSITIVE

The Consilium's editors also got plenty of practice in the revision of the orations[25] of the new Missal.

---

[24] SC 116.

[25] A liturgical prayer, commonly identified with the Collect. There are three orations at each Mass.

Of the 1182 orations in the 1962 Missal 760 were dropped entirely. Of the 422 (approximately 36 percent) that remained, the Consilium's revisers altered over half of them. So less than 20 percent of the old orations survived untouched.[26]

Father Carlo Braga, who worked on the orations, said the revisions affected "the doctrinal reality" of the prayers by incorporating "new views of human values ... ecumenical requirements ... new positions of the church" and a "new foundation of Eucharistic theology".[27] Replacing and revising texts was necessary, he said, in order that "new values, new perspectives" could be brought to light.

This meant removing or revising prayers that contained "negative theology", understood as any language that emphasized the wickedness of sin as the greatest evil and its dire consequences for the faithful both in this world and the next.[28] References to hell, death, judgement, evil, sin, the weakness of human will, concupiscence of the flesh, detachment from the world, and so on were rewritten or eliminated altogether in order to, as the old

---

[26] Quoted by Fr. Anthony Cekada, "Revised Orations: New Values, New Perspectives", YouTube video (February 25, 2012), 14:38, https://www.youtube.com/watch?v=X3PcDUZKcZw. Cf. Anthony Cekada, *Work of Human Hands: A Theological Critique of the Mass of Paul VI* (West Chester, OH: Philothea Press, 2010).

[27] Ibid.

[28] Ibid.

song goes, "accentuate the positive". According to EWTN's Father Bob Levis, "There is a new accent and emphasis found in the *Novus Ordo* which is quite foreign to almost *all* that preceded it."[29]

Considering the old axiom *lex orandi, lex credendi* (the law of prayer is the law of belief), this may go a long way to explain the short lines for Confession on Saturday and the long lines for Communion on Sunday. After all, Monsignor Bugnini himself said that "no one should find a motive for spiritual discomfort"[30] in the prayer of the Church.

Perhaps another reason is that, even with all the new Bible readings, the following verse does not appear anywhere in the new liturgy, either the New Mass or the New Office: "For any one who eats and drinks without discerning the body eats and drinks judgment upon himself."[31]

The point here is that the New Order of the Mass represents a significant change in emphasis. The old cycle of readings and the old orations grew organically in the context of the lived experience of the Church from at least the time of Pope Saint Gregory the Great. The new readings and the new prayers embody the intellectual and theological opinions

[29] "EWTN Catholic Q & A: Traditional Latin Mass and the Novus Ordo", answer by Fr. Robert J. Levis on July 28, 2002, http://www .ewtn.com/v/experts/showmessage_print.asp?number=312648 &language=en.

[30] Cekada, "Revised Orations". Cf. Cekada, *Work of Human Hands*.

[31] 1 Cor 11:29.

of a particular place and time—what Father Levis
describes as "the ecclesiology of Vatican 2".[32]

LOST IN TRANSLATION

After the actual changes, the second biggest criti-
cism of the new Missal over the past forty years is
the too-often defective English translation. Thank-
fully, two egregious examples of poor translation in
the Ordinary have been corrected in the 2010 New
Translation of the English Missal. The first is the
following oft-repeated greeting and response:

> V. *Dominus vobiscum* (The Lord be with you).
> R. *et cum spiritu tuo* (and with thy spirit).

This is how the translation appeared in every
Latin/English Missal from before Vatican II.[33] Unfortunately, the International Committee on English
in the Liturgy (ICEL) originally chose to render the
people's response "and also with you", excluding
the word "spirit" entirely.

According to the United States Conference of
Catholic Bishops website, English is the only major
language of the Roman Rite that did not translate

[32] Levis, "EWTN Catholic Q & A".

[33] Regarding "you" vs. "thy": any pre-Vatican II first-year Latin
student would point out that "you, yours" are plural whereas "thee,
thy, thine" are singular. Although these terms are more precise, modern English translations no longer make this distinction, as "thee, thy,
thine" are archaic.

the Latin word *spiritu*. They do not bother to say *why* not, but the answer lies in their website's response to a question on the corrected translation: "What do the people mean when they respond 'and with your spirit'"?

> The expression et cum spiritu tuo is only addressed to an ordained minister. Some scholars have suggested that spiritu refers to the gift of the spirit he received at ordination.[34]

Given that one of those "scholars" is Saint John Chrysostom and the language is that of Saint Paul,[35] I would call it more than a suggestion. I had to wonder, could ICEL's original translation have declined to include "spirit" in order to downplay the distinction between the ordained priesthood and the common priesthood of the faithful?

My other example of an egregious—and now corrected—mistranslation is from the Consecration of the Precious Blood. The Latin prayer recalls the words of our Lord at the Last Supper that speak of the chalice of His blood that will be poured out *pro vobis et pro multis* (for you and for many). The words "for many" are present in the biblical accounts of the Last Supper in Matthew 26:28 and Mark 14:24.

---

[34] United States Conference of Catholic Bishops, "And with Your Spirit", response to question no. 7 (2017), http://www.usccb.org /prayer-and-worship/the-mass/roman-missal/and-with-your-spirit .cfm.

[35] Cf. Gal 6:18; Phil 4:23; 2 Tim 4:22.

Yet *pro vobis et pro multis* was translated by ICEL as "for you and for *all*". Their primary justification for this deliberate mistranslation was that, whatever He may have said, Jesus died for *everyone*—"for all", not just "for many". Oddly, this was never an issue before. *The Catechism of the Council of Trent* (aka *The Roman Catechism*) plainly states:

> For if we look to its value, we must confess that the Redeemer shed His blood for the salvation of all; but if we look to the fruit which mankind have received from it, we shall easily find that it pertains not unto all, but to many of the human race.... With reason, therefore, were the words "for all" not used, as in this place the fruits of the Passion are alone spoken of, and to the elect only did His Passion bring the fruit of salvation.[36]

I guess for "modern man" the words of our Lord might be considered "a motive for spiritual discomfort in the prayer of the Church". Thanks be to God, the clear explanation of *The Roman Catechism* has been adopted by the USCCB to explain the corrected English translation.

As we've seen, from the time of Pope Saint Gregory the Great to the time of Pope Saint John XXIII, changes in the liturgy had been gradual and organic. But according to Cardinal Ratzinger,

[36] *Catechism of the Council of Trent* (Rockford, IL: TAN Books, 1982), 227.

What happened after the Council was something else entirely: in the place of the liturgy as the fruit of development came fabricated liturgy. We abandoned the organic, living process of growth and development over centuries and replaced it, as in a manufacturing process, with a fabrication, a banal on-the-spot product.[37]

Paul VI explained that promulgating the new Missal was a matter of "obedience to the Council", and its acceptance by the faithful a matter of "obedience to the Bishops".[38] With the benefit of 20/20 hindsight, it seemed plain to me that many of the liturgical changes were undertaken precisely in contradiction to the Council. It raised another question: What is true obedience, and where is it to be found?

Discovering a satisfactory answer became a matter of ongoing concern.

[37] Cardinal Ratzinger, preface to *La Reforme Liturgique en Question*, by Klaus Gamber (Le Barroux, France: Monastere Ste. Madelein, 1992). English translation: Klaus Gamber, *The Reform of the Roman Liturgy: Its Problems and Background*, trans. Klaus D. Grimm (San Juan Capistrano, CA: Una Voce Press and the Foundation for Catholic Reform, 1993), back cover.

[38] Paul VI, "Changes in Mass for Greater Apostolate" (Address to a General Audience, November 26, 1969), no. 5, taken from *L'Osservatore Romano*, Weekly Edition in English, December 4, 1969, https://www.ewtn.com/library/PAPALDOC/P6691126.HTM.

CHAPTER FIVE

THE "SPIRIT" OF VATICAN II

Long before going "Traditional", working at SJC
and watching EWTN had convinced me there
was a profound crisis of obedience in the Catholic
Church. I helped produce scores of presentations
critical of the lack of obedience among Catholics to
the Tradition of the Church, prescriptions for the
liturgy, and the authentic teaching of Vatican II.
Ironically, it was precisely appeals to the Council
or the nebulous "spirit of Vatican II" upon which
such disobedience was typically justified, encouraged, or even mandated. It seemed patently obvious
to me that this crisis of obedience was also a crisis
of authority.

Catholics do not get to pick and choose what
they believe. A Catholic who "pertinaciously denies
or doubts any of the truths which must be believed
with divine and Catholic faith"[1] commits the sin

---

[1] Fr. John Hardon, S.J., *Modern Catholic Dictionary* (Bardstown, KY:
Eternal Life 2001), 247.

of heresy. The term "heresy" comes from a Greek word meaning to "pick and choose". Formal heresy (i.e., culpably denying doctrines of the faith) carries the penalty of excommunication. Yet the fact that certain Catholic schools and universities—as well as many diocesan religious education and adult formation programs—were guilty of teaching heresy was, for me, beyond doubt. That they did so without official repercussion was similarly certain. I had a mountain of anecdotal evidence from around the country to support this conclusion and, by this point, had unfortunately experienced it firsthand in both university classes and diocesan programs.

I haven't fingers and toes enough to count the number of anathematized heresies I was subjected to by a small army of dissenting clergy, religious, and laity who, themselves having been through the soul-numbing process of modernist formation, had become like children who discover too soon there is no Santa Claus—eager to take their revenge by ruining the "innocence" of others at every opportunity. It was, in fact, the near-diabolical glee with which they scandalized the faithful that I found most disturbing.[2]

Oh, and they don't take kindly to correction. I distinctly remember the reaction of a certain Sister

---

[2] Everyone recognizes the difference between the look of delight on a teacher's face when a student "gets it" and the look of smug satisfaction when a bully succeeds in demoralizing a victim.

Mary Heretic (sorry, ex-sister)[3] when being referred to the *Catechism of the Catholic Church*. She sighed audibly and rolled her eyes in exasperation at the very *mention* of the *Catechism*.

"Oh, *that* thing?" she spat out in disgust. Then, brandishing a yellowed paperback copy of the documents of Vatican II like Arthur pulling Excalibur from the anvil, she proclaimed, "*These* documents are the *dogmas*[4] *of the Church* and *will* be … *until the next council!*"[5]

She then shared one of these temporary "dogmas" by selectively citing a passage from *Lumen Gentium* in order to demonstrate to us poor benighted fools the "infallible teaching of Vatican II" that *everyone without exception goes to heaven*! She was apparently unable to discern the none-too-subtle difference between the *possibility* of going to heaven and the *guarantee* of eternal bliss.

"The Catholic Church is like a flock of monarch butterflies," she explained; "we all go in the same general direction, *but no one is leading.*" She employed this inane metaphor to support her heretical contention that the doctrines of the Church are subject to the evolving opinions of the faithful.

---

[3] Real name withheld for prudential reasons.

[4] No dogmas were defined at Vatican II.

[5] Note the implication that Vatican II not only changed the dogmas of the Church (it didn't), but that the "next council" might change them some more (which is not possible).

"After all," she proclaimed, "the Council of Trent *added* books to the Bible."[6] This contention is demonstrably false, of course, but was put forward to suggest that past Church councils had also changed important stuff like the canon of the Bible. When I innocently asked *which* books were added, fully prepared to defend the Church's ancient acceptance of the seven books of the deuterocanon, she replied, "Oh, I don't remember ... but they *definitely* added books!" Who could argue with that?

On another occasion she declared, "The Catholic Church now admits that Martin Luther was right—*salvation is by faith alone.*" Wow. Just, wow. Once again, asked where I might find support for that new teaching, she said, "Oh, I don't know.... It was in some document.... You can probably find it online—but we *definitely* accept faith alone now!" Although Ex-Sister Mary Heretic held a doctorate in theology from a well-known Catholic university, her relentless display of ignorance and hubris was *astonishing.* I only wish I could say it was uncommon.

I can also call to mind the priestly pedagogue who insisted there should never be kneelers in a

---

[6] On the contrary, Trent defended the Old Testament canon against the Reformers' *rejection* of the seven deuterocanonical books: Baruch, Judith, 1 Maccabees, 2 Maccabees, Sirach, Tobit, and Wisdom (as well as parts of Daniel and Esther).

Catholic church because we are "a resurrected people!"[7] And I recall the deacon who demonstrated that having a "mature faith" makes it okay to question the teaching of the Church by giving the example that he personally did not believe in the doctrine of purgatory.[8]

Also, I remember another professor presbyter who sneeringly asserted that the Gospel of John is not historical—but "merely a late second- or third-century theological reflection of the 'Johannine community' "[9]—and that "all biblical scholars agree"[10] that Saint John and the Blessed Virgin Mary were *not* at the foot of the Cross!

"Gee, Father, you mean Jesus never said, 'Behold, your Mother ... behold, your son?'[11] Golly, I thought the Church considers the Bible inspired and inerrant."

"Don't be ridiculous. That *went out* with Vatican II! Everyone knows the Bible is full of falsehoods! Why, the Council specifically tells us *only those things having to do with our salvation* are 'without error.' "

[7] Kneelers might be a medieval invention as he claimed, but the practice of kneeling before our Lord is well established all the way back to the Bible (cf. Phil 2:10; Is 45:23).

[8] A fine example of heresy.

[9] This position was anathematized by Pope St. Pius X in clause 16 of his syllabus *Lamentabili Sane* (July 3, 1907).

[10] The words "all biblical scholars agree" are a red flag that whatever follows is nonsense. It has been rightly said that when you have two biblical scholars in a room, there will be at least three opinions.

[11] See Jn 19:26–27.

This particular incident took place early in my education *about* Catholic education (i.e., before I learned to keep my head down and my mouth shut), so I suggested Father was repeating an old canard based on a purposeful misreading of paragraph 11 of *Dei Verbum*, the Dogmatic Constitution on Divine Revelation. The passage in question reads:

> Therefore, since everything asserted by the inspired authors or sacred writers must be held to be asserted by the Holy Spirit, it follows that the books of Scripture must be acknowledged as teaching solidly, faithfully and without error that truth which God wanted put into sacred writings for the sake of salvation.[12]

Clearly, I argued, this does not say that *only* those things that are "for the sake of our salvation" are without error, but that *everything* which God wanted in Scripture is *without error* "for the sake of our salvation". After all, the same paragraph has only just stated:

> The books of both the Old and New Testaments in their entirety, with all their parts, are sacred and canonical because written under the inspiration of the Holy Spirit, they have God as their author and have been handed on as such to the Church herself.[13]

[12] Vatican Council II, Dogmatic Constitution on Divine Revelation *Dei Verbum* (November 18, 1965), no. 11, http://www.vatican .va/archive/hist_councils/ii_vatican_council/documents/vat-ii _const_19651118_dei-verbum_en.html.

[13] Ibid.

Father's response? "If you don't like what I'm teaching, get over it or get out." Even after these experiences, I maintain that continuing religious education—or, more precisely, *formation*—of the laity is crucial. Because, as G. K. Chesterton said, "without education we are in a horrible and deadly danger of taking educated people seriously."[14]

Case in point, the one thing all (and I mean *all*) of my diocesan and Catholic university formation classes had in common was the idea that Vatican II changed the teaching of the Church. But Ex-Sister Mary Heretic's proclamations notwithstanding, the Church's substantial comprehension of her dogmas today remains *what it has always been*. This was solemnly defined at Vatican I:

> Hence, also, that understanding of its sacred dogmas must be perpetually retained, which Holy Mother Church has once declared: and there must never be recession from that meaning under the specious name of a deeper understanding.[15]

The *Catechism of the Catholic Church* amply demonstrates that the Church's understanding of her dogmas has not changed. Our comprehension

[14] G. K. Chesterton, BrainyQuote.com, Xplore Inc., accessed June 23, 2017, https://www.brainyquote.com/quotes/quotes/g/gilbertkc 170419.html.

[15] Vatican Council I, Dogmatic Constitution on the Catholic Faith *Dei Filius* (April 24, 1870), 3.14, http://inters.org/Vatican-Council -I-Dei-Filius.

of the truth can deepen, but it can never contradict what the Church has solemnly defined.

Now, that there are sinners in the Church should not have been surprising to me. But the fact that I found dissent from the Church's solemn Magisterium—accompanied by open disrespect for the hierarchy—to be virtually *institutionalized* was deeply scandalous, *almost* as scandalous as the apathy on the part of those who might be able to do something about it. The question remained: Why do the bishops allow this situation to prevail?

IT ROLLS DOWNHILL

Any way you slice it, Catholicism is a "from the top down" proposition. Remember, the apostolic succession was the intellectual lynchpin of my conversion. Our Lord Jesus made Peter the first pope[16] and gave His Church an identifiable structure.[17] Then as now the People of God go where the leadership takes them. In my heart I felt that for a bishop to fail to correct abuses was tantamount to encouraging them: *Qui tacet consentire videtur* (Silence betokens consent).

[16] Mt 16:18–19; Jn 21:16–17.
[17] E.g., compare Jesus' twelve Apostles, the seventy-two disciples, and His inner circle of Peter, James, and John who accompanied Him up Mt. Tabor in the Gospels with the twelve young men, the seventy-two elders, and the inner circle of Aaron, Nadab, and Abihu who accompanied Moses up Mt. Sinai in the Pentateuch.

Despite fifty years of appeals to the Second Vatican Council—or the "spirit of Vatican II"—in order to justify a host of doctrinal novelties, the plain fact is, the Second Vatican Council proposed *no definitive* teachings or declarations with the authority of the extraordinary Magisterium.

There were no solemn dogmatic definitions or condemnations in the documents of the Council. The reason for this is well known: Vatican II was not called to deal with some doctrinal controversy or other, but called as a "pastoral" council examining matters of Church life, discipline, ecumenism, evangelization, and spiritual renewal. Hear the words of Pope Blessed Paul VI:

> In view of the pastoral nature of the Council, it avoided any extraordinary statements of dogmas endowed with the note of infallibility. But it still provided its teaching with the authority of the Ordinary Magisterium.[18]

So one is not free to simply *ignore* Vatican II. The ordinary Magisterium of the pope and bishops obliges the religious obedience of Catholics. However, anyone who says the Council *fundamentally changed* one or another doctrine or dogma of the Church is either mistaken or malicious. The authority of the ordinary Magisterium rests precisely in passing on what has been received. Ignoring or

[18] Paul VI, General Audience (January 12, 1966), https://www
.ewtn.com/library/papaldoc/p6691126.htm.

contradicting Church doctrine in the name of Vatican II or its ill-defined "spirit" is therefore erroneous or dishonest. The problem, in the words of Cardinal Ratzinger, is this:

> The Second Vatican Council has not been treated as a part of the entire living Tradition of the Church, but as an end of Tradition, a new start from zero. The truth is that this particular Council defined no dogma at all, and deliberately chose to remain on a modest level, as a merely pastoral council; and yet many treat it as though it had made itself into a sort of superdogma which takes away the importance of all the rest. . . .
>
> It is intolerable to criticize decisions which have been taken since the Council; on the other hand, if men make question of ancient rules, or even of the great truths of the Faith—for instance, the corporal virginity of Mary, the bodily resurrection of Jesus, the immortality of the soul, etc.—nobody complains or only does so with the greatest moderation. I myself, when I was a professor, have seen how the very same bishop who, before the Council, had fired a teacher who was really irreproachable, for a certain crudeness of speech, was not prepared, after the Council, to dismiss a professor who openly denied certain fundamental truths of the Faith.
>
> All this leads a great number of people to ask themselves if the Church of today is really the same as that of yesterday, or if they have changed it for something else without telling people. The one way in which Vatican II *can be made plausible* is to

present it as it is; one part of the unbroken, the unique Tradition of the Church and of her faith.

In the spiritual movements of the post-conciliar era, there is not the slightest doubt that frequently there has been an obliviousness, or even a suppression, of the issue of truth: here perhaps we confront the crucial problem for theology and for pastoral work today.[19]

This is the foundation of what Benedict XVI called the "hermeneutic of continuity".[20] Put simply, Vatican II must be understood in the context of the Tradition of the Church; the Tradition of the Church should not be reinterpreted in light of Vatican II.

But the prevailing narrative, without which the Council is simply incomprehensible to many, is that Vatican II *was* a break with Tradition and a "new start from zero". Whether you consider that a good thing or a bad thing depends on your point of view. What I failed to realize is, what was true for Ex-Sister Mary Heretic was true for the Traditionalists as well.

[19] Joseph Cardinal Ratzinger, Address to the Bishops of Chile (Santiago, July 13, 1988), http://unavoce.org/resources/cardinal-ratzingers -address-to-bishops-of-chile/.

[20] Benedict XVI, post-synodal apostolic exhortation *Sacramentum Caritatis* (February 22, 2007), note 6 (in note 6, Pope Benedict refers readers to his Address to the Roman Curia on December 22, 2005, when he uses the phrases "hermeneutic of discontinuity and rupture" and "hermeneutic of reform"), http://w2.vatican.va/content/benedict-xvi /en/apost_exhortations/documents/hf_ben-xvi_exh_20070222 _sacramentum-caritatis.html.

CHAPTER SIX

SAINT INCOGNITO

As the retirement date for our pastor at Saint Anonymous approached, the bishop unexpectedly declared that the Indult Mass had been allowed only for the sake of our elderly priest and not, in the words of Saint John Paul II, to "facilitate" the "ecclesial communion" of the faithful, nor to "guarantee respect for their rightful aspirations".[1] Therefore, the bishop decreed, when our pastor retired, the Traditional Mass would retire with him.

As you might suspect, I considered this dreadful news. Hundreds of Catholics from all over our diocese were to be deprived of the Traditional Latin Mass by episcopal fiat, appeals to papal instructions for its "wide and generous application"[2] notwithstanding.

The volume of people who attended the final Traditional Latin Mass at Saint Anonymous made

---

[1] John Paul II, apostolic letter *Ecclesia Dei* (July 2, 1988), no. 5, http://w2.vatican.va/content/john-paul-ii/en/motu_proprio/documents/hf_jp-ii_motu-proprio_02071988_ecclesia-dei.html.

[2] Ibid., no. 6.

the front page of the local newspaper. Betty and baby Emmy were in the photograph that accompanied the article—the rest of us couldn't get a seat. I considered it a great injustice that the bishop would take away this Mass, especially as a local order of religious priests volunteered to keep it going. It was, in a word, devastating. In Matthew 13:44 our Lord says,

> The kingdom of heaven is like *treasure* hidden in a field, which a man found and covered up; then in his *joy* he goes and sells all that he has and buys that field.

My family and I had discovered the treasures of the Traditional liturgy, and the idea that we would have to go back to the self-congratulatory banality that marked the typical *Novus Ordo* Mass in our diocese was daunting to say the least. Then a "miracle" occurred.

THE ANSWER TO A PRAYER?

Feeling cast adrift by the bishop's decision, I wondered where we would assist at Mass. I had already seen what the diocesan authority foisted on the congregation at Saint Ubiquitous when their pastor retired—and he was only moderately conservative. I shuddered to think what was in store for Saint Anonymous, having been home to the local "Trad" community. I was not the only one to experience this anxiety, of course. "To whom shall we go?" became the hot topic at coffee and doughnuts. One Sunday, weeks before our pastor's final Traditional Mass, a fellow parishioner inquired where we lived. When I replied, she asked, "Why don't you go to the Traditional chapel there?" I said I did not know there was one.

She then informed me that a local homeschooling co-op had acquired an old Protestant school campus—complete with a chapel—where they established a Traditional Catholic charter school *and* offered a *daily Traditional Mass*! The chapel, which we'll call Saint Incognito, was located just ten minutes from our house. What an incredible discovery. It seemed too good to be true, so I decided to investigate.

Saint Incognito Chapel was a small, modest building, but richly appointed. I assisted at a weekday Low Mass, celebrated with devotion and attention to detail. When it was over I thought, "Everything here is perfect, with one obvious exception: As a convert cum lay apologist, how can I possibly bring my family to a chapel outside the diocesan structure?"

After all, I was employed by a conservative Catholic media apostolate. I was a public figure with my own reputation to consider as well as Saint Joseph's—not to mention the possibility of causing scandal and potentially losing the job that supported my growing family. Working for SJC *and* attending an Independent chapel seemed irreconcilable.

But as I wrestled with the apparent impossibility of this course of action, I could not ignore the fact that for weeks I had been earnestly praying to our Lady to provide just such a place for us to continue assisting at what I was beginning to consider the "true Mass". Could it be a mere coincidence that a Traditional chapel had suddenly appeared right in my own back yard?

A "Valid" Question

Before going any further, I inquired about the situation of the "pastor" at Saint Incognito. I discovered that Father Perennis[3] had been duly ordained in a Vatican-approved priestly institute dedicated to the Traditional Mass and Sacraments. For all anyone seemed to know, he was a priest in good standing. Having been sent to the United States with a superior of his society, Father Perennis had apparently "blown the whistle" on some "irregular activities". His superior was subsequently indicted and punished for his crimes. As a reward, Father Perennis was reportedly cut off without explanation. After years at SJC, this type of incident had become a familiar story to me. It seemed that here was just another case of an upright, orthodox priest ordered to await a "next assignment" that simply never came.

[3] Real name withheld for prudential reasons.

Caught in this "holding pattern", Father Perennis accepted the invitation to celebrate the Traditional Latin Mass for the community at the new chapel. I resolved to get the whole story "from the horse's mouth", if only Betty would agree to come to the chapel at all. Everything hinged on that. I would not try to force her into a decision that would conflict with her conscience.

I should also say that I was genuinely concerned for my children. Betty and I could go back to the *Novus Ordo* and grit our teeth, but what about the kids? Although I had no issue with the New Mass itself, I considered the poor translation, common abuses, heterodox homilies, and generally lax atmosphere a real and present danger to the faith of my children. After all, Pope John Paul II's oft-repeated call for a "new evangelization",[4] and even the very existence of lay apostolates like Saint Joseph Communications, were predicated on the undeniable fact that, since Vatican II, Catholics had abandoned their faith by the millions worldwide.

In my tacit capacity as in-house apologist at SJC, I dealt virtually every day with phone calls and e-mails from brokenhearted parents trying to figure out why their kids left the Church. At the time, statistics suggested that only about 15 percent

[4] John Paul II, encyclical *Redemptoris Missio* (December 7, 1990), no. 33, http://w2.vatican.va/content/john-paul-ii/en/encyclicals/docu ments/hf_jp-ii_enc_07121990_redemptoris-missio.html.

of young adults continued to attend Church after Confirmation. There had to be a reason why 85 percent of them forsook the faith of their fathers. Despite many contributing factors, I considered ill-conceived attempts to make the liturgy more "relevant" to be at the top of the list.

After much prayer and deliberation, I managed to convince myself that concern for the salvation of my family justified attending Saint Incognito. I knew the Mass to be valid, because it was an approved rite celebrated by a duly ordained priest. However, I also knew, since the chapel was not in communion with the local ordinary, the Mass was not licit. But, then again, the questionable liceity of our diocesan *Novus Ordo* Masses is what got me started down this path to begin with.

In my mind, the question boiled down to this: Should we attend a beautiful, reverent, valid, but illicit, Traditional Latin Mass, or attend a valid *Novus Ordo* Mass probably rendered illicit through relentless, imbecilic, not to mention scandalous, liturgical abuse? To ask the question was to answer it. I simply felt I had no choice.

WHAT ABOUT BETTY?

What really concerned me now was Betty. Could a "solid, orthodox" cradle Catholic be content with such a situation? I well knew that the same misgivings were in her mind as in my own, and no doubt some others as well. I had attended a weekday Mass at Saint Incognito and liked what I saw. Would she be willing to come on Sunday? Would she reserve judgment until after we had been there together as a family? She agreed.

When Sunday came, I thought back to Betty's reaction when I first took her to Saint Anonymous: "I feel like I've just been to Mass for the first time." What would her response be now? After that initial Sunday Mass at Saint Incognito, I could not even wait to get outside to find out. Still in the vestibule, I asked her, "Well?" Betty looked up at me and said, "I feel like I'm home." As a wave of relief, excitement, and I do not know what else washed over me, little Mary Grace stopped in her tracks and said out loud, "Do you smell that? It smells like roses." Apparently given the stamp of the "odor of sanctity", I, too, felt that in this humble place I was finally home.

Real Community

After becoming "parishioners" at Saint Incognito, one of the first things Betty and I did was invite Father Perennis to dinner. At his suggestion, we met him at a restaurant with a reputation for fine prime rib. When he arrived wearing his cassock, half of my apprehensions about attending the chapel vanished. Clerical dress is a practical symbol of the Catholic faith, and it can have a powerful impact when worn "in the world". I admit I had always been somewhat scandalized by the many *Novus*

Ordo priests I knew who habitually abandoned their clerics once off parish grounds. Wearing his cassock was a more eloquent testimony of his commitment to the Church than any words he might have said. On that score, Father simply shared an unadorned account of how he came to be "pastor" at Saint Incognito. No excuses, no recriminations, just the facts. We were satisfied.

The weeks and months that followed were an invigorating time, and I thanked our Lord and His Blessed Mother constantly. At last I was able to attend daily Mass without distraction, heretical homilies, or fear of liturgical abuse. The chapel itself was a genuine source of joy as I knelt, stood, and sat in an atmosphere of quiet reverence surrounded by traditional Catholic appointments.

In many ways, even more than Saint Anonymous, the Independent chapel looked like a Catholic church, with its stately high altar, centrally located tabernacle, beautiful crucifix, and traditional statues of the Sacred Heart, the Blessed Virgin Mary, Saint Joseph, Saint Michael, the Infant of Prague, and others. During our first spring there they installed superb stained glass windows. Because it was a formerly Protestant "worship space", there were no kneelers at first, but this was hardly daunting to a congregation eager to kneel before the Presence of the Lord even if it meant, for the time being, kneeling on the floor.

Best of all, after the Mass itself, was the congregation. At Saint Anonymous, "ordinary" parishioners

would sometimes attend the Indult Mass at noon
and bring their casual attire and casual behavior with
them. Occasionally, a couple of elderly women
would show up in jeans and sneakers and chat audibly throughout the Mass. Being near the coast,
there was always some guy there in flip-flops and
shorts—and girls in even less—as well as vacationers
who treated the picturesque little church more like
a curious tourist attraction than a place of worship.

What a difference at Saint Incognito! Everyone
assisted in reverent silence. Everyone dressed appropriately. Women unfailingly covered their heads.[5]
Every Mass (including the three celebrated each
Sunday) was preceded by a communal Rosary. At
Low Masses, after the Last Gospel,[6] Father would
lead the Prayers after Low Mass.[7] And, once Father

[5] Head covering for women was mandated by canon 1262 of
the 1917 Code of Canon Law. Although there is contention about
whether canons are still in force that have not been specifically abrogated, canon 1 of the 1983 Code states that its publication abrogates
the 1917 Code.

[6] After the blessing at the end of the Traditional Mass, the priest
turns to the left side of the altar to read the Last Gospel (Jn 1:1–14). The
priest and the people genuflect together at the words *Et Verbum caro
factum est* (And the Word was made flesh) in honor of the Incarnation.

[7] Prescribed by Pope Leo XVIII in 1884 for recitation by the priest
and the people, the Prayers after Low Mass, or Leonine prayers, con-
sisted of three Hail Mary's, the Hail Holy Queen (Salve Regina), followed by a versicle and response, a prayer for the conversion of sinners
and the liberty and exaltation of the Catholic Church, the Prayer to
Saint Michael the Archangel, and, lastly, the invocation "Most Sacred
Heart of Jesus, have mercy on us", recited three times. The official
intentions for which the Leonine prayers were recited changed over
time, until they were suppressed in 1965.

and the servers had exited, the whole congregation would recite the Anima Christi, the Prayer before a Crucifix, and an Our Father, Hail Mary, and Glory Be for the intentions of the pope. On Sundays, Mass was followed by the customary coffee and doughnuts accompanied by good fellowship.

And there were families—lots and lots of young families who cared deeply about the religious upbringing of their many children. We established friendships and supported one another, rejoicing with those who rejoiced and weeping with those who wept.[8] It was, in a word, a genuine community: a group of devoted people of all ages and ethnicities bound by the bonds of Christian charity. They understood that Mass is a time to worship God and that "building community" happens organically in real relationships between people of like mind and heart. It is not something that can be imposed from above or run by committee. When I lost my position at SJC, this community—priests and people—supported my fledgling apostolate of Pro Multis Media[9] and kept us going. In the weeks, months, and years that followed, my family became firmly attached to the Saint Incognito community.

But I continued to struggle with my decision. Perhaps what troubled me most was the nagging

[8] Cf. Rom 12:15.

[9] For further information about the apostolate, see the home page of Pro Multis Media at http://promultismedia.net/.

question: Why me? Why can I see all this while others cannot? Why can't my friends and colleagues connect the dots? On the other hand there was the ever-present knowledge that, whatever my justifications, *good* Catholics are obedient to their bishop.

On this front, the chapel gift shop offered a selection of books and tapes on liturgy, spirituality, theology, and the like, all written from a Traditionalist perspective. I became familiar with the positions of Professor Dietrich von Hildebrand,[10] Michael

---

[10] Dietrich von Hildebrand (October 12, 1889–January 26, 1977) was a pioneer of the Catholic Traditional Movement, a professor at Jesuit Fordham University, and the founder of the Roman Forum—a nonprofit organization dedicated to the broad defense of Catholic doctrine and culture. Pope Pius XII informally dubbed Dr. von Hildebrand "the twentieth-century Doctor of the Church". Roman Forum, "About", http://www.romanforum.org/about/. Also held in high regard by post-conciliar popes Saint John Paul II and Benedict XVI, he was nevertheless an outspoken critic of the changes in the Church following Vatican II, especially the new liturgy.

His academic reputation lent gravity to the Traditionalist interpretation of the Church after Vatican II. For instance, to the charges of "legalism" and "disobedience" often lodged against Traditional Catholics he wrote: "But in truth a greater, more real legalism has come into being since the Second Vatican Council.... The belief that a lack of discipline is more serious than the spread of heresies is a typical form of legalism. All disciplinary authority, all obedience to the bishop presupposes the pure teaching of the holy Church. Obedience to the bishop is grounded in complete faith in the teachings of the holy Church. As soon as the ecclesiastical authority yields to pluralism in questions of faith, it has lost the right to claim obedience to its disciplinary ordinances." Dietrich von Hildebrand, *The Devastated Vineyard*, trans. John Crosby and Fred Teichert (Harrison, NY: Roman Catholic Books, 1985), 19.

Davies,[11] and others—not to mention Archbishop
Marcel Lefebvre.[12]

These materials, along with certain Traditionalist periodicals and websites, would greatly influence
my opinions on the legitimacy—perhaps even the
necessity—of "resisting" diocesan authority when it
could be deemed harmful to the salvation of souls.

[11] Michael Davies (March 13, 1936–September 25, 2004) was a
Welsh Catholic school teacher and prolific author of many Traditionalist books and booklets. In his three-volume *Liturgical Revolution*
series—*Cranmer's Godly Order* (1976), *Pope John's Council* (1977), and
Pope Paul's New Mass (1980)—Davies argued that the changes made
in the Traditional Mass since Vatican II not only went beyond what
that Council authorized, but, in some cases, actually contradicted it.
He proposed that the New Order of the Mass constituted a revolution
rather than a reform and that this revolution had produced no good
fruits to compensate for its destruction of the Catholic liturgical inher-
itance. From 1996 to 2003, he served as president of the International
Federation Una Voce, which allowed him access to the Congregation
for the Doctrine of the Faith, the Congregation for Divine Worship
and the Discipline of the Sacraments, and the Pontifical Commission
Ecclesia Dei.

[12] See the next chapter for more information on Archbishop Marcel
Lefebvre.

CHAPTER SEVEN

THE INFLUENCE OF THE SOCIETY OF SAINT PIUS X (SSPX)

The Society of Saint Pius X (SSPX) is a Tradition-alist group that continues to wield great influence among Traditional Catholics of all stripes. According to Cardinal Ratzinger:

> We must reflect on this fact: that a large number of Catholics, far beyond the narrow circle of the Fraternity of Lefebvre, see this man as a guide, in some sense, or at least as a useful ally.[1]

Considering the undeniable impact of Archbishop Lefebvre and his priestly fraternity on the Traditional Movement as a whole, I suspect a little history is in order.

In October 1967, the previously mentioned Consilium (*Consilium ad exsequendam Constitutionem de Sacra Liturgia*, the Consilium for Implementing

---

[1] Joseph Cardinal Ratzinger, Address to the Bishops of Chile (Santiago, July 13, 1988), http://unavoce.org/resources/cardinal-ratzingers-address-to-bishops-of-chile/.

the Constitution on the Sacred Liturgy) produced a complete draft of the "Normative Mass", which was presented to the Synod of Bishops in Rome. They attended the first public celebration of this Mass at the Sistine Chapel. Asked to vote on the new liturgy, seventy-eight bishops voted *placet* (approved), forty-three voted *non placet* (not approved), and sixty-two voted *placet juxta modum* (approved with reservations). In response to the apparent lack of approval, the Normative Mass was replaced by the text of the New Order of the Mass in 1969.[2]

In September 1969, a little more than a year before the New Mass became obligatory, Cardinals Alfredo Ottaviani and Antonio Bacci sent Pope Paul VI a letter accompanied by a Short Critical Study of the New Order of the Mass. This study, better known today as the "Ottaviani Intervention", was prepared the previous June by twelve theologians under the direction of Archbishop Marcel Lefebvre.[3]

Highly critical of the new liturgy, the "Ottaviani Intervention" contended that the New Order of the Mass represented "both as a whole and in its

[2] Alfredo Cardinal Ottaviani and Antonio Cardinal Bacci, *The Ottaviani Intervention: Short Critical Study of the New Order of Mass*, trans. Anthony Cekada (Rockford, IL: TAN, 1992), 31.

[3] Holy Cross Seminary, Most Asked Questions about the Society of Saint Pius X, Appendix III, Short History of the Society of Saint Pius X, transcription of a conference given by Rev. Fr. Ramón Anglés (reprinted from the *Angelus*, January 1996), http://holycrossseminary .com/Most_Asked_Questions_Appendix_III_page2.htm.

details, a striking departure from the Catholic theology of the Mass as it was formulated in Session XXII of the Council of Trent"[4] and claimed that on many points the New Mass had much "to gladden the heart of even the most modernist Protestant".[5]

Pope Paul VI sent the study to the Congregation for the Doctrine of the Faith (CDF). In November 1969 the CDF responded that it contained affirmations that were "superficial, exaggerated, inexact, emotional and false".[6] Cardinal Ottaviani for his part stated in 1970:

> I have rejoiced profoundly to read the Discourse by the Holy Father on the question of the new Ordo Missae, and especially the doctrinal precisions contained in his discourses at the public Audiences of November 19 and 26 [1970] after which I believe, *no one can any longer be genuinely scandalized.* As for the rest, a prudent and intelligent catechesis must be undertaken to solve some legitimate perplexities which the text is capable of arousing.[7]

[4] Ottaviani and Bacci, *Ottaviani Intervention*, 27.

[5] Ibid., 33.

[6] Christophe Geffroy and Philippe Maxence, *Enquête sur la messe traditionnelle* (La Neff, 1998), 21; cited in *Wikipedia*, s.v. "Ottaviani Intervention", last modified June 23, 2017, https://en.wikipedia.org /wiki/Ottaviani_Intervention.

[7] Letter from His Eminence Alfredo Cardinal Ottaviani to Dom Gérard Lafond, O.S.B., in *Documentation Catholique* 67 (November 1970): 215–16, 343, quoted in James Likoudis and Kenneth Whitehead, *The Pope, the Council and the Mass* (Steubenville, OH: Emmaus Road, 2006), 143–44; first published in 1981 by Christopher Publishing House (W. Hanover, MA).

Nonetheless, the "Ottaviani Intervention" remains an influential document in Traditionalist circles, and Archbishop Marcel Lefebvre emerged as probably the most significant figure in the Traditionalist Movement.

Lefebvre founded the Society of Saint Pius X (SSPX) *ad experimentum* in 1970. Organized as a *pia unio* (pious union) dedicated to the Traditional Mass and Sacraments, the SSPX ceased to be recognized as an organization within the Catholic Church after a Vatican-ordered apostolic visit in 1975.[8] Yet, with an estimated six hundred thousand adherents, the SSPX remains the largest Catholic Traditionalist group operating outside the canonical structure of the Church today.[9] While I personally had no official association with the SSPX,[10] there is no denying that the Society was highly influential among those Traditionalists estranged from the diocesan structure.

In 1988, Archbishop Lefebvre—renouncing an agreement that he had already signed[11]—ordained

---

[8] *Wikipedia*, s.v. "Society of Saint Pius X", last modified July 24, 2017, https://en.wikipedia.org/wiki/Society_of_Saint_Pius_X. See also François Charrière, Decree of Erection for the Priestly Society of St. Pius X (November 1, 1970), http://sspx.org/en/sspxs-founding -documents. (At the time, François Charrière was bishop of Lausanne, Geneva, and Fribourg.)

[9] Society of Saint Pius X, "General Statistics about the SSPX", accessed July 9, 2017, http://sspx.org/en/general-statistics-about-sspx.

[10] Full disclosure: my family never attended SSPX chapels or schools, but two of my children were confirmed by visiting SSPX bishops.

[11] Ratzinger, Address to the Bishops of Chile.

four Society priests to the episcopate *without the required papal mandate*. The Holy See considered this a schismatic act for which Lefebvre and the four newly ordained bishops[12] were judged automatically excommunicated.[13] Subsequent ordinations by the four SSPX bishops are therefore illicit, and the priests they ordain automatically suspended. The excommunications did not extend to the faithful who attend SSPX chapels.

Although the excommunications of the four bishops were lifted by Pope Benedict XVI in 2009, he reiterated that the SSPX still "does not possess a canonical status in the Church" and its clergy "do not exercise legitimate ministries in the Church".[14] Bishop Robert Morlino of the Madison, Wisconsin, diocese recently elaborated on the current situation of the Society:

> [The SSPX's] relationship with the Church is complex and developing. Moreover, the situation of SSPX bishops, of SSPX priests, of the faithful who formally align themselves with the SSPX, and of the faithful who occasionally or informally

[12] Those consecrated as bishops were Bernard Fellay, Bernard Tissier de Mallerais, Alfonso de Galarreta, and Richard Williamson.

[13] John Paul II, apostolic letter *Ecclesia Dei* (July 2, 1988), no. 3, http://www.vatican.va/roman_curia/pontifical_commissions/ecclsdei/documents/hf_jp-ii_motu-proprio_02071988_ecclesia-dei_en.html.

[14] Letter of His Holiness Pope Benedict XVI to the Bishops of the Catholic Church concerning the Remission of the Excommunication of the Four Bishops Consecrated by Archbishop Lefebvre (March 10, 2009), http://w2.vatican.va/content/benedict-xvi/en/letters/2009/documents/hf_ben-xvi_let_20090310_remissione-scomunica.html.

attend Mass with the SSPX, are all different in important ways. It would be inaccurate to call it a schismatic group in a strict sense, and we should all pray that it may someday be fully reconciled with the Church.[15]

Bishop Morlino charitably stated his belief that "many of [SSPX's] concerns are legitimate", their "values and aspirations are admirable", and their zeal "impressive". He also called upon the faithful of his diocese to be "cordial, respectful, and welcoming" to SSPX adherents as "brothers and sisters in Christ".[16] But he sounds a note of caution regarding an important issue. Although he concedes that SSPX Masses are valid, the Sacraments of Matrimony and Penance require faculties from the local ordinary (bishop). Without the necessary faculties, conferred by legitimate authority, the SSPX's marriages and absolutions are not merely illicit but invalid.[17] This was the very issue I wrestled with at Saint Incognito.

---

[15] Bishop Robert Morlino, "A Word of Caution about the Society of Saint Pius X", *Diocese of Madison Catholic Herald*, August 6, 2015.

[16] Ibid.

[17] Pope Francis had graciously granted SSPX priests faculties for hearing confessions for at least the duration of the Year of Mercy (December 8, 2015 to November 20, 2016). At this writing, he "personally decided to extend this faculty beyond the Jubilee Year". Francis, apostolic letter *Misericordia et Misera* (November 20, 2016), no. 12, http://w2.vatican .va/content/francesco/en/apost_letters/documents/papa-francesco -lettera-ap_20161120_misericordia-et-misera.html.

CHURCH SUPPLIES

Following the lead of the Society, the priests at the Independent chapel addressed the issue of necessary faculties with an appeal to "supplied jurisdiction". Canon law states that the salvation of souls is the supreme law (*salus animarum suprema lex*);[18] therefore, in certain cases, the Church supplies (*Ecclesia supplet*) the necessary priestly faculties for the good of the faithful. Bishop Morlino notes, "The SSPX argues for the validity of their marriages and absolutions based on the canonical principle that the Church supplies the faculty *in cases of doubt or common error.*"[19]

Specifically, the Church supplies jurisdiction when the faithful think a priest has a jurisdiction that he does not have;[20] when there is a probable and positive doubt that the priest has jurisdiction;[21] when a priest inadvertently continues to hear confessions once his faculties have expired;[22] and when the penitent is in danger of death—and then even if the priest is laicized or an apostate.[23] The SSPX's conclusion?

[18] Can. 1752.
[19] Morlino, "Word of Caution about the Society of Saint Pius X".
[20] Can. 144.
[21] Ibid.
[22] Can. 142 §2.
[23] Can. 976; 1335. Cf. Society of Saint Pius X, SSPX FAQs, Question 9: "Do Traditional Priests Have Jurisdiction?" (2013), http://archives.sspx.org/SSPX_FAQs/q9_supplied_jurisdiction.htm.

Now, the nature of the present crisis in the Church is such that the faithful can on good grounds feel it a moral impossibility to approach priests having ordinary jurisdiction. And so, whenever the faithful need the graces of penance and want to receive them from priests whose judgment and advice they can trust, they can do so, even if the priests do not ordinarily have jurisdiction. Even a suspended priest can do this for the faithful who ask: "for any just cause whatsoever" (canon 1335).[24]

SSPX and Independent Traditional priests therefore cite what they perceive to be the "emergency situation" in the Church (i.e., poor catechesis, modernism, liturgical abuse, etc.) to justify setting up their own apostolate over and against the local ordinary, for which, they argue, "the Church" supplies the necessary faculties. But even if the faithful are truly ignorant of their priests' lack of faculties, that does not absolve SSPX priests from presenting themselves as if they had them.

Besides, the pope (who is the supreme legislator) and the bishops in communion with him clearly do not consider the Church in a state of emergency— not the least because no one is being *denied* the Sacraments. Alleged "moral impossibilities" aside, Penance, Matrimony, and other Sacraments of certain validity are readily available through diocesan ministries at local parishes.

---

[24] Society of Saint Pius X, SSPX FAQs, Question 9.

What did all this mean to me? Well, I did not scruple to seek absolution from diocesan priests even after I started attending the Traditionalist chapel. But a situation involving a young couple who wanted to get married at Saint Incognito made me really stop and think.

When the couple insisted they would not be married in a *Novus Ordo* ceremony, the bride's parents took it upon themselves to arrange for a Traditional Latin Nuptial Mass at their diocesan parish. As you might imagine, this was no simple task. I advised the couple to accept the offer and frankly expected them to leap at the chance, if only for the sake of future family unity. The priests at the chapel also understood the prudence of this course of action and said as much. My young friends ultimately chose to get married at Saint Incognito anyway, despite the dubious validity of the Sacrament of Matrimony officiated by a priest without faculties. Having introduced them to the Independent chapel to begin with, I felt a certain responsibility.

MATTHÆUM CONTRA MUNDUM

As in-house apologist for Saint Joseph Communications, I pursued a certificate in Christian counseling because I recognized that most ex-Catholics leave the Church over moral issues or hurt feelings. Their doctrinal objections tend to proceed from an intellectual attempt to justify what was at root an emotional decision. Sadly, knowing this does not make you immune to it. The point being, whatever the objective reality, Traditionalists typically do not consider themselves to have abandoned the Church. If anything, they feel as if the Church has abandoned them. Cardinal Ratzinger explained it this way:

> Schisms can take place only when certain truths and certain values of the Christian faith are no longer lived and loved within the Church. The truth which is marginalized becomes autonomous, remains detached from the whole of the ecclesiastical structure, and a new movement then forms itself around it.[25]

The faithful who are marginalized for being "too Catholic" naturally gravitate to such movements. But what then? Unfortunately, as Bishop Morlino points out:

> You might attend your first Mass at an SSPX chapel for good and noble reasons, e.g., such a strong initial desire for a reverently celebrated liturgy that you are willing to tolerate the SSPX's irregular status. But as you attend more and more, it ceases to become something you tolerate and starts to become a mark of identity, even a badge of pride. You adopt a fixed posture of separation

[25] Ratzinger, Address to the Bishops of Chile.

from the Church. That is a perilous position for
any soul to be in.[26]

I recall how this was brought home to me in a
powerful way. In January 2002, Pope John Paul II
established the Personal Apostolic Administration of
Saint John Mary Vianney for Traditionalist Catholics within the Diocese of Campos, Brazil. Whereas
the jurisdiction of the local ordinary of Campos
is territorial, Bishop Fernando Arêas Rifan, as apostolic administrator, exercises jurisdiction only over
particular persons in the same diocese. This personal
apostolic administration is the only Catholic Church
jurisdiction devoted exclusively to celebrating the
Traditional Mass and Sacraments.

I met Bishop Rifan at a conference sponsored
by a local chapter of Una Voce America in 2004.
His presentation on the apostolic administration was
truly inspirational. Here, I thought, was the very
model for Traditionalist reconciliation with the
Church. A day after the event I asked Father Perennis what he thought of the possibility of such an
arrangement here in the United States. His response
caught me completely off guard. He simply asked,
"Why would I want to be under a bishop?"

I was scandalized. "Why would you want to be
under a bishop? Because that's how Jesus set up
the Church," I thought. Surely this attitude was a

[26] Morlino, "Word of Caution about the Society of Saint Pius X".

far cry from "I'm just waiting for my next assignment." And then the little voice inside my head
said, "Yeah, but *you're* here too, aren't you? How
comfortable have *you* become with not being in
full communion with the Church?"

I began to see that the longer "a fixed posture
of separation from the Church" lasts, the deeper
one's rationalization must become in order to justify
continuing to hold the position. Bishop Rifan
addressed this very point when responding to the
objection that yearly he would have to concele-
brate a *Novus Ordo Missae* in his role as a bishop in
full communion with Rome. After affirming that
"the rite of Paul VI *is* the official rite of the Latin
Church,[27] celebrated by the Pope and by *all* the
Catholic episcopate", Bishop Rifan warned:

> If we consider the New Mass in itself, in theory
> or in practice, as invalid or heretical, sacrilegious,
> heterodox, sinful, illegitimate or not Catholic, we
> would have to hold the theological conclusions
> of this position and apply them to the Pope and
> the entire episcopate residing in the world—that
> is, the whole teaching Church: that the Church
> has officially promulgated, maintained for decades,
> and offers every day to God an illegitimate and
> sinful worship—a proposition condemned by the

---

[27] This was before Benedict XVI offered his clarification in *Summorum Pontificum* that the Traditional Mass and New Mass are not two
rites, but two *forms* of the *one* Roman Rite.

Magisterium—and that, therefore, the gates of hell have prevailed against her, which would be a heresy. Or else we would be adopting the sectarian principle that we alone are the Church, and outside of us there is no salvation, which would be another heresy. These positions cannot be accepted by a Catholic, either in theory or in practice.[28]

This certainly described where many of the Traditionalists I knew were headed if they weren't there already—including, maybe, me.

[28] "Bishop Rifan Answers Questions about Alleged Concelebration", Una Voce, accessed June 24, 2017, http://www.uvoc.org/bishop_rifan_answers_questions_.htm.

Chapter Eight

Excuses, Excuses

One of the most rewarding things about my years at Saint Joseph Communications was helping folks find their way into the Catholic Church. I recall a lengthy dialogue with a certain Evangelical Protestant. It started with a question about the papacy. I cleared up some misconceptions, shared some Bible verses, and directed him to some solid resources. I encouraged him to keep seeking, assured him of my prayers, and expected that to be that. But over the course of the next several months he continued to call regularly. I kept answering his questions from a biblical and historical perspective and directing him to good resources as his intellectual objections fell like dominoes.

His final hurdle was the hardest for many non-Catholic Christians to overcome: the Church's teaching on Mary. We went back and forth until he called to say, "Okay, I can accept Mary as Mother of God, her Perpetual Virginity, even her Immaculate Conception—but the Assumption, though, I just don't know. I can't really find anything about it in

the Fathers until the end of the second century—"
and then I snapped.

"Your problem isn't the Assumption," I said.
"Your problem is you don't want to be Catholic. In
your heart you already know the truth. You're just
looking for excuses not to convert. Don't bother
calling me again until you're serious." And I hung
up. I instantly regretted what I had done, but I
didn't have his number—or even his last name—so
there was no taking it back.

Nearly a year later, I was emceeing a biblical
conference with Scott Hahn and Jeff Cavins when
a fellow came up and introduced himself as the guy
from the phone calls. I apologized for my rudeness
when we last spoke, but he said it was just what he
needed to hear. He had flown to the conference
from another state to tell me in person that since that
last phone call he had stopped looking for excuses
and been received into the Catholic Church. Then
he shared "the rest of the story".

What I could not have known was that this fellow was not merely an Evangelical Protestant but
a pastor with his own church. On top of that, he
was part owner of a chain of Christian bookstores
for which he was contractually obliged to profess
the Reformation principles of *sola scriptura* and *sola
fides*.[1] So, coming into the Catholic Church meant

---

[1] I.e., that the *Bible alone* is the sole rule of faith and that salvation
is by *faith alone*.

giving up his vocation, his livelihood, and, for the most part, his friends—not to mention what it put his family through. I could relate.

The moral of the story is simple: the spiritual benefits of full communion with the Church come with a price—namely, submission to legitimate authority—and sometimes that means giving up a lot. I was being reminded that I had made such a sacrifice myself. Frankly, it made me feel like a bit of a fraud. In the year it had taken this fellow to come into full communion with the Church, I had chosen to step outside the diocesan structure.

Like the guy from the phone calls, many Traditionalists find themselves looking for excuses not to return to full communion with the Church, perhaps without even realizing it. A turn-of-the-millennium book published by the SSPX provides a powerful example. I think it is worth a closer look to see how their arguments hold up—in light of not only the true teaching of Vatican II, but Traditional sources as well.

THE PROBLEMS WITH *THE PROBLEM*

The letter from Cardinals Ottaviani and Bacci that accompanied the 1969 "Ottaviani Intervention", prepared by "a group of theologians" under the direction of Archbishop Marcel Lefebvre, stated that the New Order of the Mass represents "both as a whole and in its details a striking departure from the Catholic theology of the Mass as it was formulated in Session XXII of the Council of Trent".[2] The citation here refers to Trent's infallible teaching that the Mass is a propitiatory sacrifice—one that appeases the wrath of God and satisfies for our sins.[3]

Thirty-two years later, the SSPX produced a book called *The Problem of the Liturgical Reform: A Theological and Liturgical Study*,[4] wherein the above charge is reaffirmed by another anonymous group of experts—this time not "theologians", but "pastors of souls" allegedly "qualified in theological, liturgical and canonical matters".[5] Since they are anonymous this is impossible to verify.

Many, if not most, Traditionalist works are defensive—arguments about how Trads are not really disobedient or schismatic. But this book takes the offensive against "post-conciliar" theological and liturgical orientations and purports to prove the New Mass is unacceptable because it is essentially the fruit of a *new religion*. *The Problem* is divided into three parts and makes three basic claims:

[2] Alfredo Cardinal Ottaviani and Antonio Cardinal Bacci, *The Ottaviani Intervention: Short Critical Study of the New Order of Mass*, trans. Anthony Cekada (Rockford, IL: TAN, 1992), 27.

[3] *Council of Trent*, Session XXII, chapter II.

[4] Society of Saint Pius X, *The Problem of the Liturgical Reform: A Theological and Liturgical Study* (Kansas City, MO: Angelus Press, 2001).

[5] Bishop Bernard Fellay, introduction to ibid., ii.

1. The New Mass constitutes a liturgical rupture with Tradition.
2. The New Mass is based on a new theology of sin and redemption that the authors call the "theology of the Paschal Mystery".[6]
3. "Paschal Mystery theology" stands condemned by traditional Catholic doctrine.

A thorough repudiation of all the claims made in *The Problem of the Liturgical Reform* is quite beyond the scope of this little book as it would take a book twice the length of the original to repropose and then refute all the arguments contained therein. It is made the more difficult because the SSPX are often "wrong for all the right reasons". But even when they get the facts straight, the desire to justify their continued separation from full communion with Rome colors their *interpretation* of the facts. I hope it will suffice to point out some of the flaws in their main theses.

Paschal Mystery

What is the Paschal Mystery, and is it really incompatible with traditional Catholic doctrine? According to Father John Hardon's *Modern Catholic Dictionary*, "Paschal Mystery is a general term to describe the redemptive work of Christ, especially

---

[6] Ibid., iv.

the events of the Last Supper and Passion, reaching their climax on Easter Sunday."[7] No problem so far. The glossary of the *United States Catholic Catechism for Adults* states:

> In speaking of the Paschal Mystery we present Christ's death and Resurrection as one, inseparable event. It is *paschal* because it is Christ's passing into death and passing over it into new life. It is a *mystery* because it is a visible sign of an invisible act of God.[8]

The anonymous SSPX authors admit the term can be found in the writings of the Fathers of the Church. Yet they claim the theology of the Paschal Mystery is a novelty that "minimizes the mystery of the Redemption", "alters the sacrificial dimension of the Mass", and renders "the post-conciliar liturgy dangerously distant from Catholic doctrine".[9] Commenting on *The Problem*'s theory in a lecture on the theology of liturgy, Cardinal Ratzinger said:

> This rupture is seen precisely in the fact that everything is interpreted henceforth [i.e., after Vatican II] on the basis of the "paschal mystery," instead of the redeeming sacrifice of expiation of Christ; the

[7] Fr. John Hardon, S.J., *Modern Catholic Dictionary* (Bardstown, KY: Eternal Life, 1999), 405.

[8] United States Conference of Catholic Bishops, *United States Catholic Catechism for Adults*, s.v. "Paschal Mystery" (Washington, D.C.: USCCB Publishing, 2006), 522–23; italics in original.

[9] Fellay, introduction to *Problem of the Liturgical Reform*, ii.

category of the paschal mystery is said to be the heart of the liturgical reform, and it is precisely that which *appears* to be the proof of the rupture with the classical doctrine of the Church. It is clear that there are authors who lay themselves open to such a misunderstanding; but *that it is a misunderstanding is completely evident* for those who look more closely.[10]

The Problem of the Liturgical Reform relies heavily on quotations from "authors who lay themselves open" to misinterpretation. This is obviously not the best way to represent the official teaching of the Church. Individual theologians do important work, and that work can inform the Magisterium, but it does not dictate to it or replace it. The official interpretation of the teachings of Christ and the Apostles belongs to the Church, and I was taught the place to seek a concise presentation of that official teaching is the *Catechism of the Catholic Church* (*CCC*). In *Fidei Depositum*, Pope Saint John Paul II affirmed that the *Catechism* is intended for use by *all the Christian faithful*, and declared it to be "a sure norm for teaching the faith".[11] Therefore, it may

[10] Joseph Cardinal Ratzinger, "Theology of Liturgy" (lecture delivered during the *Journees liturgiques de Fontgombault*, July 22–24, 2001), trans. Margaret McHugh and Fr. John Parsons, http://www.pierced hearts.org/benedict_xvi/Cardinal%20Ratzinger/theology_liturgy .htm.

[11] John Paul II, apostolic constitution *Fidei Depositum* (October 11, 1992), section IV, "The Doctrinal Value of the Text", http://w2 .vatican.va/content/john-paul-ii/en/apost_constitutions/documents /hf_jp-ii_apc_19921011_fidei-depositum.html.

be no coincidence that the SSPX can be every bit as dismissive of the *Catechism* as left-leaning diocesan instructors. And for the same reason: it is less open to misinterpretation. Consider the following from the *Catechism of the Catholic Church* in light of the SSPX's accusation about the "Paschal Mystery" contradicting Traditional doctrine:

> Christ's death is both the *Paschal sacrifice* [italics in original] that accomplishes the *definitive redemption* of men, through "the Lamb of God, who takes away the sin of the world" (Jn 1:29; cf. 8:34–36; 1 Cor 5:7; 1 Pet 1:19), and the *sacrifice of the New Covenant* [italics in original], which restores man to communion with God by *reconciling him to God* through the "blood of the covenant, which was poured out for many for the forgiveness of sins" (Mt 26:28; cf. Ex 24:8; Lev 16:15–16; 1 Cor 11:25).[12]

The *United States Catechism for Adults* calls Jesus' sacrifice on the Cross "an act of atonement", an "*act of satisfaction* or *reparation*", and "an *expiation* for our sins".[13] Sounds an awful lot like the Traditional doctrine.

The SSPX rightly points out that the Council of Trent solemnly defined Christ's great act of self-giving on the Cross as a propitiatory sacrifice. The problem comes when they contend that "the

---

[12] *CCC* 613.

[13] *United States Catholic Catechism for Adults* (Washington, D.C.: United States Conference of Catholic Bishops, 2006), 92, italics in original.

theology of the Paschal mystery . . . no longer wishes to consider the Passion of Christ as a propitiatory offering to divine justice offended by sin."[14]

Does the "post-conciliar Church" really wish to *deny* propitiation or to *explain* it? When I was in RCIA, I was certainly taught that "sin is an offense against God."[15] Further, I was taught to pray in the Act of Contrition, "I detest all my sins because of *Your just punishments*, but most of all because *they offend You*, my God . . ." In this common prayer, recited daily by millions of Catholics, we specifically acknowledge the divine justice offended by sin. *Lex orandi, lex credendi.*

THE WRATH OF GOD

Propitiation refers to appeasing God's wrath. The Bible speaks specifically of the wrath of God more than forty times.[16] But it speaks also of His love as the specific motivation for our redemption.[17] Biblically speaking, God's wrath is a given, but so is His love for sinners. How then do we reconcile His acceptance of a sacrifice to appease His wrath with His infinite goodness, love, and mercy? Not surprisingly, the wrath of God is not *like* our wrath.

---

[14] *Problem of the Liturgical Reform*, 40.

[15] *CCC* 1850.

[16] I understand that if you count up all the biblical allusions to God's anger, you'll find nearly six hundred references.

[17] Jn 3:16.

For my thoughts are not your thoughts, neither
are your ways my ways, says the Lord. For as the
heavens are higher than the earth, so are my ways
higher than your ways and my thoughts than your
thoughts.[18]

God is eternal and immutable (unchanging). He
is not happy one day and angry the next. References to His "wrath" in the Bible are like references to His "right hand" or His "holy arm" or His
"footstool". God the Father does not have arms,
hands, or feet[19] any more than He has human pas-
sions. But the inspired authors of the Bible employ
such anthropomorphic language because metaphor
and poetry can often express profound truths more
comprehensibly than even the most comprehen-
sive prose.

"The wrath of God", then, is a figure of speech,
but one that points to the reality of how unrepentant
sinners experience God's justice, which is insepara-
ble from His love. Since sinners reject both, they
experience God's love and justice as *wrath*—like a
fire that burns instead of warms. But God does not
stop loving the sinner or even love him less. God the
Father did not have millennia's worth of stored-up
rage to pour out on His Son on Calvary, nor did He

[18] Is 55:8–9.
[19] St. Thomas Aquinas, *Summa Theologica* I, q. 1, a. 10, ad 3, http://
www.documentacatholicaomnia.eu/03d/1225-1274,_Thomas
_Aquinas,_Summa_Theologiae_%5B1%5D,_EN.pdf.

need to exact vengeance on mankind. But if that is the case, then what happened on the Cross?

COVENANT REPRESENTATIVE

According to the SSPX's representation of Paschal Mystery theology, "the need to satisfy divine justice is no longer apparent, and the doctrine of the *vicarious satisfaction* of Christ appears scandalous."[20] But how can this be when the "post-conciliar" Church, rather than being "scandalized", *defines* Christ's sacrifice on the Cross in terms of His love giving it value precisely as "redemption and reparation, as atonement and *satisfaction*", according to the *Catechism*?[21] The *Catechism* goes on to say,

> No man, not even the holiest, was ever able to take on himself the sins of all men and offer himself as a sacrifice for all. The existence in Christ of the divine person of the Son, who at once surpasses and embraces all human persons and constitutes himself as the Head of all mankind, makes possible his redemptive sacrifice *for all*.[22]

Jesus' sacrifice was not a mere *substitution* like the ram sacrificed in the place of Isaac.[23] In addition, as Joseph Cardinal Ratzinger affirms, Jesus' sacrifice is

[20] *Problem of the Liturgical Reform*, 42.
[21] *CCC* 616.
[22] Ibid.; italics in original.
[23] Cf. Gen 22:1–19.

"representative" and "participatory".[24] If an innocent person is executed for a guilty person's crimes, the guilty person is still guilty. But when we say Jesus died for us, we mean He died, not only in our place, but on our behalf—not simply as our substitute, but as our *covenant representative*.

In the Old Testament, Adam is our first covenant representative. His representation and our participation are like the father of a family and his children. If the father of a family is rich, his children will inherit his fortune. If he is destitute, his children will inherit his debt. So Adam's *fall* is representative and participatory because through it we all inherit Original Sin when we are born into the human family. Jesus came into the world as a new Adam whose *sacrifice* is representative and participatory because through it we are all redeemed and may inherit eternal life when we are *born again*[25] as the adoptive children of God.

What happened on Calvary was not a revelation of a wrathful God visiting vengeance on His innocent Son. God did not look down on the Cross and see only our sins and blindly pour out His rage on His Son. Rather, He looked with love upon the perfect love and obedience of His Son, who,

[24]Joseph Cardinal Ratzinger, "Vicarious Representation", trans. Jared Wicks, S.J., in *Letter and Spirit*, vol. 7 of *The Bible and the Church Fathers: The Liturgical Context of Patristic Exegesis* (Steubenville, OH: Emmaus Road, 2011), 209–20.

[25]Jn 3:5.

to summarize the above quote from the *Catechism*, paid a debt He did not owe because we owed a debt we could not pay.

In Eden, God wanted Adam, our first covenant representative, to obey Him from loving trust in His perfect will, but Adam refused. Christ, our New Covenant representative, offered that loving trust to the Father on the Cross. Having taken on our human nature in the Incarnation, Jesus offered His life in loving obedience to the Father.[26] When Jesus gave up His spirit, water and blood flowed from His side,[27] as a visible sign of the invisible mysteries of Baptism and the Eucharist. Through His sacrifice we receive God's life through the Sacraments. Hear the voice of the Church:

> The cross is the unique sacrifice of Christ, the "one mediator between God and men" (1 Tim 2:5). But because in his incarnate divine person he has in some way united himself to every man, "the possibility of being made partners, in a way known to God, in the paschal mystery" is offered to all men (GS 22 § 5; cf. § 2). He calls his disciples to "take up [their] cross and follow [him]" (Mt 16:24).[28]

Through the Sacraments, we participate in Jesus' act of atonement and satisfaction and receive the grace He merited for us so that we may take up our own

[26] Cf. Jn 15:13.
[27] Jn 19:34; cf. 1 Jn 5:6.
[28] *CCC* 618.

crosses and fill up "what is lacking in Christ's afflictions for the sake of his body, that is, the Church".[29] This is not a new teaching; this is the Good News: "But God shows his love for us in that while we were yet sinners Christ died for us."[30]

Through the Cross, God reveals a divine mercy that does not compromise divine justice. On the Cross, the love of Christ overcomes our sins. If Adam's (and our) sin is a rejection of divine sonship, Christ's atoning, representative sacrifice is its ultimate expression. It is a reassertion of filial love that defeats sin at its source: our proud and foolish refusal to love and trust our Father as His children.

SACRIFICE OR MEMORIAL MEAL?

On a related topic, the SSPX claims a close analysis of the New Mass and says that the General Instruction of the Roman Missal (GIRM 2) "compels us to recognize that the structure of the rite is no longer based on *sacrifice* but on a *memorial meal*".[31] Further, they claim:

> The key to explaining the mystery of the Mass is no longer the Cross but the Last Supper, which has become the prime model for the rite when considered as a memorial meal.... The fundamental

[29] Col 1:24.
[30] Rom 5:8.
[31] *Problem of the Liturgical Reform*, 3.

difference between the traditional missal and the new missal [is this]; in the former, the Mass is a sacrificial offering of the transubstantiated presence of Christ, while in the latter the Mass is understood as a memorial of Christ's Passover.[32]

The question then is, does the Church really affirm that the New Mass is no longer a sacrifice but merely a memorial meal? It does not seem so:

The Eucharist is the *very sacrifice* of the Body and Blood of the Lord Jesus which he instituted to perpetuate *the sacrifice of the cross* throughout the ages until his return in glory. Thus he entrusted to his Church this memorial of his death and Resurrection. It is a sign of unity, a bond of charity, a paschal banquet, in which Christ is consumed, the mind is filled with grace, and a pledge of future glory is given to us.[33]

In what way then is the Eucharist a memorial of the sacrifice of Christ?

The Eucharist is a memorial in the sense that it *makes present and actual the sacrifice which Christ offered to the Father on the cross*, once and for all on behalf of mankind. The sacrificial character of the Holy Eucharist is manifested in the very words of institution, "This is my Body which is given for you" and "This cup is the New Covenant in my Blood that

[32] Ibid., 11–12.

[33] *Compendium of the Catechism of the Catholic Church*, no. 271 (cf. *CCC* 1322–23; 1409).

will be shed for you" (Luke 22:19-20). The sacrifice of the cross and the sacrifice of the Eucharist *are one and the same sacrifice* [italics in original]. The priest and the victim are the same; only the manner of offering is different: in a bloody manner on the cross, in an unbloody manner in the Eucharist.[34]

This certainly seems consistent with the traditional doctrine to me.

Where some folks get it wrong is in thinking that Jesus instituted a meal at the Last Supper while his sacrifice on Calvary was a completely separate event. "Jesus did not redeem us with beautiful words, but with his suffering and death," said Cardinal Ratzinger in the Jubilee Year 2000. "His Passion gives power to his words.... Whoever omits the cross omits the essence of Christianity."[35] And if you omit the Eucharist, you omit what explains how Christ's death became the means for our salvation.

I dare say the majority of the witnesses on Calvary that first Good Friday did not comprehend the Crucifixion as a sacrifice, but an execution. How was the execution of Jesus transformed into the supreme sacrifice? The answer is to be found in the Cenacle on Holy Thursday. Jesus did not simply celebrate the Passover (Pasch) one last time or institute a mere

---

[34] Ibid., no. 280 (cf. *CCC* 1362–67).

[35] Joseph Cardinal Ratzinger, Address on the New Evangelization, at the Jubilee of Catechists (December 12, 2000), quoted in Scott Hahn, *Evangelizing Catholics: A Mission Manual for the New Evangelization* (Huntington, IN: Our Sunday Visitor, 2014), 154.

memorial meal. As the fulfillment of the Lamb of God, He transformed the Old Testament Passover into the Passover of the New Testament.

At crucial moments of the Last Supper, Jesus departed from the traditional words and actions of the Jewish Passover. When He broke the bread, He spoke the words, "This is my body."[36] Then, at the end of the meal, He took the third cup of blessing and pronounced, "This is my blood of the covenant, which is poured out for many."[37] The Apostles could not have failed to be surprised by this, or by what happened next. Instead of proceeding to the fourth cup of the Passover after singing "the great Hallel",[38] Scripture says that after singing the hymn, "they went out to the Mount of Olives."[39] There Jesus entered into His Passion with the prayer, "My Father, if it is possible, let this chalice pass from me; nevertheless, not as I will, but as thou wilt."[40]

On Calvary His blood *was* poured out. On the Cross Jesus, the High Priest, offered Himself as *the* sacrifice of the New Covenant. It was only after saying, "I thirst,"[41] and drinking the sour wine that Jesus proclaimed, "It is finished."[42] What is finished?

[36] Mt 26:26; Mk 14:22; Lk 22:19.
[37] Mt 26:28; Mk 14:24; cf. Lk 22:20.
[38] Ps 136.
[39] Mt 26:30.
[40] Mt 26:39.
[41] Jn 19:28.
[42] Jn 19:30.

The Passover liturgy. Some biblical exegetes spec-
ulate that it is the Passover liturgy that was finished
with Jesus' acceptance of the final cup that He so
dreaded in the Garden.

It was after this act of loving obedience to God's
will that Christ could say, "Father, into your hands
I commit my spirit!"[43]

That the Last Supper and the Cross are *two* parts
of *one* event is foreshadowed by the Old Testament
Passover. The Pasch wasn't simply a meal. It started
as a sacrifice and culminated in a meal. As always,
what was true of the Old Testament type is not less
true but even more true of the New Testament fulfillment. Jesus came as the Lamb of God not just
to feed us, but to die for us. If the Last Supper was
merely a meal, then Jesus' death on the Cross was
just an execution. But Jesus' institution of the Holy
Eucharist was more—it was the institution of the
New Covenant Passover sacrifice. That is what
transforms the events of Good Friday into a holy
sacrifice. But how is that sacrifice transformed into
a Sacrament?

NOT JUST A SACRIFICE

The mystery of the Eucharist transforms Jesus'
bloody sacrifice into a holy sacrifice; but it is the

---

[43] Lk 23:46 (cf. Ps 31:5).

Resurrection that transforms His sacrifice into a Sacrament. This brings us to the final SSPX objection. They claim Paschal Mystery theology implies "the principal act of Redemption is no longer the death of Christ but His Resurrection and his Ascension."[44] For proof they cite the section of the General Instruction of the Roman Missal that affirms, "The Passion and the Resurrection are equally the object of this memorial meal,"[45] and, "These two mysteries are, moreover, united in a single expression; in this memorial, Christ instituted the 'Paschal meal'.... The expression 'Paschal sacrifice' is also used."[46]

They go on to admit, "The Resurrection certainly *contributes* to our salvation, notably as an example for us, but classic theology maintains that only the death of Christ—and not His Resurrection—has a meritorious and satisfactory value. Thus for classic theology, it is the Passion rather than the Resurrection which sums up our salvation."[47] Finally, the authors conclude, "The new theology increasingly empties the classic conception of the Eucharistic sacrifice by maintaining that the sacrifice of Christ cannot consist of His death alone, but must necessarily include His Resurrection and Ascension."[48]

[44] *Problem of the Liturgical Reform*, 4.
[45] GIRM 2.
[46] Ibid., 56, 335.
[47] *Problem of the Liturgical Reform*, 76.
[48] Ibid., 79.

Once again the SSPX authors are asserting too much and not enough. Firstly, what is the importance of the Paschal Mystery of Jesus in the "post-conciliar" teaching of the Church?

> The Paschal Mystery of Jesus, which comprises his passion, death, resurrection, and glorification, stands at the center of the Christian faith because God's saving plan was accomplished once for all by the *redemptive death* of his Son Jesus Christ.[49]

So far so good, but the SSPX is not only claiming that the principle act of redemption is Christ's death, but that the Resurrection, while *contributing* to our salvation, is not strictly necessary nor to be considered a part of the redemption. Saint Paul has a different idea. He tells us that the Resurrection was necessary because it is the means by which we die and rise to new life in Christ:

> We were buried therefore with him by baptism into death, so that as Christ was raised from the dead by the glory of the Father, we too might walk in newness of life.... So you also must consider yourselves dead to sin and alive to God in Christ Jesus.[50]

In Romans 4:25, Saint Paul says Jesus "was put to death for our trespasses and was raised for our

---

[49] *Compendium of the Catechism of the Catholic Church*, no. 112 (cf. CCC 571–73).
[50] Rom 6:4, 11.

justification", and, in 1 Corinthians 15:17, "if Christ has not been raised, your faith is futile and you are still in your sins." Jesus' death is not the only aspect of His saving work. Our salvation requires both the payment rendered on the Cross for the debt of our sin and Jesus' Resurrection for the sake of our justification. Christ's Resurrection was not merely for His own sake, but that mankind might be united to His divinity.

In an article from the SSPX publication *SiSi-NoNo*, someone with the pen name Ermenegildus declares the "Resurrection was the fruit of [Christ's] Passion.... His resurrection was earned, and not praiseworthy," but, because of Paschal Mystery theology, "Good Friday is eclipsed by Resurrection Sunday, the glorious *reward* being substituted for the sorrowful *meriting*."[51] Once again we see the claim that while the Resurrection may have a place in our salvation, it is *not necessary for our redemption*. Compare that to the teaching of the *Catechism*—not the 1992 *Catechism of the Catholic Church*, but the 1566 *Catechism of the Council of Trent*:

> Finally, the Resurrection of our Lord, as the pastor should inculcate, was *necessary* to complete the mystery of our salvation *and redemption*. By His

[51] Ermenegildus, "Pius XII and Paschal Mystery Theology", *SiSi-NoNo*, April 30, 2002, trans. Suzanne Rini for *The Angelus*, http://www.sspxasia.com/Documents/SiSiNoNo/2002_September/Pius_XII.htm.

death Christ liberated us from sin; by His Resurrection, He restored to us the most important of those privileges which we had forfeited by sin. Hence the words of the Apostle: He was delivered up for our sins and rose again for our justification. That nothing, therefore, may be wanting to the work of our salvation it was necessary that as He died, He should also rise again.[52]

This is not the only pre-conciliar text that refutes the SSPX. In the popular 1874 work *The Holy Sacrifice of the Mass* by Father Michael Muller, C.Ss.R., the learned priest devotes a chapter to the Mass as a sacrifice of propitiation, but two chapters to the Mass as the renewal of Christ's Resurrection. But what about the Traditional Mass itself?

The Offertory of the Traditional Mass includes the prayer *Suscipe, sancta Trinitas*, which mentions the "death, resurrection and ascension" of our Lord. Likewise after the Consecration at the *Unde et memores* the Roman Canon proclaims: "In memory of the blessed Passion of the same Christ, Thy Son, our Lord, of his resurrection from the place of the dead, and of his ascension into the glory of heaven". If this is not a reference to the Paschal Mystery, it will certainly do until one comes along. The point is, with all the riches and profundity of the Traditional Mass, why insist its meaning be summarized

[52] *Catechism of the Council of Trent* (Rockford, IL: TAN Books, 1982), 70.

exclusively as "the death of Christ" when it is so much more? Jesus' Resurrection and glorification are what makes it possible for us to partake of His sacred humanity. It is the resurrected Lord who comes to us in the Eucharist.

A SINGLE DROP

I remember reading an article from an Evangelical writer giving a list of reasons "why Jesus *had* to die". But that is contrary to the understanding of the Catholic Church. Jesus prayed to the Father, if it were possible to let the cup of suffering pass from Him.[53] Could it have passed? The Church's answer is yes. One drop of Jesus' Precious Blood would have been enough to redeem the whole human race. One act of obedience by the Son was all it would have taken. But Jesus gave much more than that, not because it was necessary, but because it was fitting: "Greater love has no man than this, that a man lay down his life for his friends."[54]

"The Cross," says Pope Benedict, "reminds us that there is no true love without suffering, there is no gift of life without pain."[55] Jesus instituted the Sacrament of love on Holy Thursday, on Good

[53] Mt 26:39.

[54] Jn 15:13.

[55] Benedict XVI, General Audience (September 17, 2008), http://w2.vatican.va/content/benedict-xvi/en/audiences/2008/documents/hf_ben-xvi_aud_20080917.html.

Friday He endured the suffering of love, and on Easter Sunday He gave the gift of love that provides mankind with the Sacrament that enables us to love and share in a life that is truly divine. It is because of the Resurrection that we can become "partakers of the divine nature"[56] at the Holy Mass.

> The Eucharist is the memorial of Christ's Passover, that is, of the work of salvation accomplished by the life, death, and resurrection of Christ, a work made present by the liturgical action.[57]

After more than a hundred pages of the most radical accusations, in the end, the authors of *The Problem of the Liturgical Reform* were obliged to admit, however grudgingly, "Certainly, the reformed missal does not deny Catholic dogma outright."[58] While some of their accusations may hold true for certain theologians, they are handily refuted by recourse to the *Catechism*. The teaching of the Church regarding redemption has not changed. But it must be appreciated that the Magisterium of the Church is a living office, an ongoing responsibility to make the deposit of faith comprehensible to each generation. Catholics are not "Bible alone" Christians, but we cannot be "Council of Trent alone" Christians either.

[56] Cf. 2 Pet 1:14.
[57] *CCC* 1409.
[58] *Problem of the Liturgical Reform*, 100.

Coming full circle, I wonder, could the motivation for this exercise have been primarily an attempt by the SSPX to legitimize their continued refusal of full communion with Rome? Is this the all-too-predictable consequence of adopting a fixed posture of separation from the Church?

STATUS REPORT

In 2008, the four bishops of the SSPX approached Pope Benedict to request that he lift their 1988 excommunications. Excommunication is an ecclesiastical censure by which a person is more or less excluded from communion with the faithful. It prohibits a cleric from exercising a legitimate ministry in the Church. The Society has argued from the beginning that the 1988 sentence of excommunication was unjust and constituted a main obstacle to their return to unity with Rome. In January 2009, Pope Benedict generously remitted the excommunications for the same reason that they had been imposed in the first place: "namely, to invite the four Bishops once more to return".[59] In other words, the serious sentence of excommunication was meant to reveal the gravity of Archbishop

[59] Letter of His Holiness Pope Benedict XVI to the Bishops of the Catholic Church concerning the Remission of the Excommunication of the Four Bishops Consecrated by Archbishop Lefebvre (March 10, 2009), http://w2.vatican.va/content/benedict-xvi/en/letters/2009 /documents/hf_ben-xvi_let_20090310_remissione-scomunica.html.

Lefebvre's act of disobedience to the pope, hopefully helping the newly made SSPX bishops to realize the necessity of their return to the fold. Likewise, lifting the excommunications was intended as a gesture of generosity proposed in order to bring about that same desired unity.

However, despite the reactions of some bishops, the press, and certain proponents of the SSPX suggesting that, for good or for ill, lifting the excommunications changed the Society's standing in the Church, Benedict XVI made it clear that the remission did not alter the canonical status of the SSPX. It was rather a matter of a mercy granted to individual persons who requested it, not a change in the standing of the SSPX institution: the excommunications were lifted, but the SSPX is still not in full communion.

Further, Pope Benedict made it clear that the remaining obstacles to their return to full communion are doctrinal rather than disciplinary. Therefore, inasmuch as the Pontifical Commission *Ecclesia Dei*[60] is responsible for "those communities and persons who, coming from the Society of Saint Pius X or from similar groups, wish to return to full communion with the Pope",[61] Benedict XVI turned

---

[60] The Pontifical Commission *Ecclesia Dei* was established by Pope John Paul II in his apostolic letter *Ecclesia Dei*, given motu proprio. For further explanation of the commission, see the beginning of chapter 10 below.

[61] Letter of Benedict XVI concerning the Remission of Excommunication.

over management of the commission to the Congregation for the Doctrine of the Faith. "This will make it clear that the problems now to be addressed are essentially doctrinal in nature."[62] So, while the SSPX are not considered by the Holy See to be in formal schism, the reasoning that their stance of "resistance" is merely a matter of Church discipline is no longer justifiable.

As for me, the thing I love most about Catholicism is that, of all the competing worldviews ever proposed to me, it is the only one that consistently makes sense. The teachings of the Catholic Church all fit together to form a cohesive whole in keeping with the promise of her Divine Founder: "He who hears you hears me."[63] I can still hear the echo of Father Magister: "Don't talk to *me* about it. These are the teachings of Jesus." My concern with the SSPX's view was a contradiction I found at its heart. If their claim is, "We're just following Tradition," then when was it ever "traditional" to adopt a fixed position of opposition to the ordinary Magisterium? At what time did "following Tradition" ever mean that Independent priests, excommunicated bishops, and a host of lay Catholics get to decide for themselves which teachings and laws promulgated by the Vicar of Christ and the bishops of the world are binding and which are not?

[62] Ibid.
[63] Lk 10:16.

I did not share the SSPX's doctrinal objections in the first place. Therefore, upon deeper reflection, my rationalizations for being outside the diocesan structure began to erode as well. When I broached the subject of returning to the diocesan structure with my wife, she responded by arranging a private meeting with Father Perennis so he could "talk me down". Father did not impart any deep insight or pertinent factor I had not already considered. Needless to say I was neither convinced nor comforted by our little get-together; still, I was not at all sure I could suffer the "slings and arrows" of the typical *Novus Ordo* Mass. Even though I was no longer satisfied with the customary justifications for remaining outside full communion, I felt like I had "made my bed and must now lie in it". Frankly, I am not sure where I would be today were it not for the fact that our Lady was about to take a hand.

Chapter Nine

Our Lady to the Rescue

Although my devotion to the Blessed Virgin Mary began even before my Baptism, I never associated myself with any particular Marian apparition. The primary reason was the almost daily e-mails, letters, and phone calls that came in to SJC filled with apocalyptic warnings, messages, and prophecies from the devotees of a host of dubious private revelations. Of course, even approved apparitions and private revelations are not part of the deposit of faith—and they too can support a fringe element. I was perfectly satisfied with my daily Rosary.

Then, shortly before the turn of the century, someone sent me an e-mail about Our Lady of Good Success. I was skeptical. First off, the title Our Lady of Good Success sounded like some kind of Catholic version of the "health and wealth Gospel". Secondly, I couldn't seem to find out anything about it through the usual channels. When I learned my cradle Catholic wife's Italian mother had never even *heard* of this devotion, I assumed it must not be legit and let it drop.

Fast-forward to one morning after Mass at Saint Incognito: I was in the chapel gift shop when lo and behold, I discovered a couple of books about Our Lady of Good Success and the visionary Mother Mariana de Jesus Torres. Knowing Betty's love for Mary, and that she was unfamiliar with the devotion, I gave the books to her for Mother's Day 2006. She too was skeptical at first, but changed her tune after reading the books. We learned that devotion to Mary of Good Success was, in fact, approved by the Church and, further, the official cause for Mother Mariana's beatification had been opened.

Later that year I was "downsized" from SJC. After plenty of prayer, Betty and I determined to start our own Traditional Catholic media apostolate. I wanted to take Mary as our patroness, of course, and Betty suggested we place the new company, Pro Multis Media, under the mantle of Our Lady of Good Success.

The Statue and the Message

In 1599, Mary appeared to Mother Mariana with the request to commission a statue of herself holding the Infant Jesus in one hand and a crozier and the keys to the convent in the other. Mary said the crozier and keys were meant to represent that she (Mary) was to be considered the sisters' true and perpetual Abbess. Then she told Mother Mariana, "In my left arm place my divine Child: so that men will understand how powerful I am in obtaining mercy and pardon for every sinner.... They should come to me for I shall lead them to him."[1] Simply put, "To Jesus through Mary".

The many miracles associated with the image began with the completion of the statues. The sculpture was undertaken by a local artist but, according to Mother Mariana, was miraculously completed by the archangels Michael, Gabriel, and Raphael under the direction of Saint Francis of Assisi.

But the most intriguing part of the story to me was the many prophecies our Lady made about the Church and the world in the nineteenth and twentieth centuries. Mary told Mother Mariana that there would be a great crisis of faith and morals in the Church and that the world would reach a critical stage after the midpoint of the twentieth century. And what happened at this time? I was there. We call it "the sixties". Mother Mariana relates that when our Lady granted her a vision of these times, if she had not been miraculously sustained, the shock would have killed her. In the course of seven apparitions over a period of forty years, our Lady revealed many prophecies to Mother Mariana, including the following:

> There will be an almost total and general corruption of customs.... Innocence will no longer

[1] Matthew Arnold, *Mary of Good Success and the Restoration of the Church* (Garden Grove, CA: Pro Multis Media, 2012), 10.

be found in children nor modesty in women.... The Sacrament of Matrimony will be attacked and iniquitous laws will make it easy to live in sin.... The effects of secular education will be one reason for the lack of religious vocations.... Wealthy and powerful Catholics will stand by and witness the oppression of the Church, the persecution of virtue, and the triumph of evil without employing their resources to oppose evil and restore the Faith....[2] In this supreme moment of need of the Church, those who should speak will fall silent.[3]

With prophecies like these (and many more) it is easy to see why Traditionalists would seize upon this apparition as an indictment of the "post-conciliar Church". However, the thing that attracted me most about Mary's message for our times was that it doesn't end with the gloomy predictions. On the contrary, in an obvious reference to Genesis 3:15,[4] Mary foretold that the apparent triumph of evil in our days "will mark the arrival of my hour, when I, in a marvelous way, will dethrone the proud and cursed Satan, trampling him under my feet".[5] The original postulator for the cause for the beatification of Mother Mariana, the late Monsignor Luis

[2] Cf. ibid., 28–35.

[3] Matthew Arnold, *Our Lady of Good Success Pamphlet* (Garden Grove, CA: Pro Multis Media, 2007), 3.

[4] "I will put enmities between thee and the woman, and thy seed and her seed: she shall crush thy head, and thou shalt lie in wait for her heel" (DRV).

[5] Arnold, *Mary of Good Success*, 35.

Cadena y Almeida, Chaplain of Honor to His Holiness John Paul II, commented in his 1991 book *Mensaje Profetico* (*The Prophetic Message*) that all the prophecies of Mary of Good Success have been fulfilled, save one—the promised restoration of the Catholic Church.

Buen Suceso, which we translate "good success", literally means a "great event" or perhaps, more dynamically, a "happy ending". Now I ask you, what is the happy ending for a Christian? Heaven, of course. But how often is heaven attained only after much suffering? When I asked this question to a group of priests and seminarians at Holy Apostles Seminary in Cromwell, Connecticut, octogenarian professor Father Bill McCarthy shouted out, "Always!" I am inclined to agree. But considering that all the other prophecies of Our Lady of Good Success have been fulfilled to the letter— and remember, we're talking prophecies made four centuries ago—we have good reason to hope the marvelous restoration will come to pass as well.

An Unexpected Journey

A month or so after founding Pro Multis, Betty and I discovered a Traditional priest we knew was going on pilgrimage to the Convent of the Immaculate Conception in Quito, Ecuador, where the apparitions took place. Betty said I should pack my camera and microphone and head for Ecuador to make a documentary on Our Lady of Good Success.

Naturally, my passport was expired, not to mention the fact that I did not even know if I would be permitted to take so much as a snapshot in any of the churches down there. Plus, Pro Multis was barely off the ground, and we were in debt up to our eyeballs. I told Betty it didn't seem like good timing. She said Mary wanted me to go. I had already learned never to say no when my wife and the Blessed Mother gang up on me.

When I got to Quito, I discovered my anxieties about shooting video there were unfounded. Everyone was friendly and accommodating, and I was even allowed to go into the cloister and interview the erstwhile Mother Abbess, Madre Ines Maria del Sagrario. In fact, while I was setting up the shot, Madre Ines said, through an interpreter, "We've been waiting for you."

Like everywhere else, the Church in Ecuador is fighting secularism, but many of the locals I encountered clearly had the Catholic faith. Some of the peasant people I met asked, "Who's your saint?" like Americans used to ask, "What's your sign?" in the seventies.

One day I visited the convent's "clinic" in order to make a donation for some devotional items. I expected sisters in nurse's uniforms giving immunization shots to wide-eyed children. Instead, I passed through a metal door into a small open courtyard with a single stone bench. A blackboard hung on one wall that listed suggested donations for the available remedies (mostly herbal teas) as well as holy cards, pictures of Our Lady of Good Success, and third-class relics of Mother Mariana. The transactions were made through a lazy Susan–type affair (it is a cloister after all), so I never saw the sister who took my donation. There were a couple of locals in the courtyard: a grandmother and a young girl waiting for the sisters to prepare an herbal remedy. They motioned to see my picture of our Lady. "Oh, muy bonita!" said the old woman. Kissing her fingers, she touched the faces of Mary and the Infant Jesus and encouraged the little girl to follow her example. It was a tender moment.

But for all the inspirational experiences I had in Quito, the most significant came when I visited the convent church alone, just to be in the presence of our Lord in the Blessed Sacrament and the miraculous statue. I knelt down and prayed for a while and then was silent. I simply told Mary, "Well, I'm here ..." I don't know what I expected, really. I certainly had no visions, but I did "hear" an interior voice say, "People here have the faith, but the only Traditional Mass in Quito is the one you brought with you."[6] As I pondered this revelation, I experienced the overwhelming impression that I needed to get myself and my family back into full communion with the Church.

I don't know for sure that it was our Lady, but the incident had a definite impact on me. I thought

---

[6] The priest who acted as our chaplain celebrated the Traditional Latin Mass on the altars of the magnificent baroque churches we visited.

about the fact that, with all she said about the twentieth century, Mary of Good Success made no mention of the *Novus Ordo Missae*. Somehow *Mary* was able to operate within the institutional Church. Could the Mother of God be happy that some of her devotees had taken a more or less permanent stance of resistance to the Church's hierarchy—even to the point of setting up an independent apostolate over and against their local bishops while yet claiming to be "loyal to the pope"?

Our Lady's one recorded instruction in Scripture is, "Do whatever he tells you."[7] How do we know what Jesus is telling us to do? According to the *Baltimore Catechism*, Jesus teaches us through the Catholic Church[8]—specifically through the Apostles and their successors, the bishops. Jesus said, "He who hears you hears me, and he who rejects you rejects me, and he who rejects me rejects him who sent me."[9] Pretty simple, really. But as you and I both know, *simple* doesn't necessarily mean *easy*—especially when it comes to obedience.

Traditional Catholics are quick to point out the Church's approval of this apparition to lend credence to the fact that Mary prophesied a crisis of faith and morals in our times. Some especially point to the 1991 "canonical coronation" of the statue of Our Lady of Good Success by Antonio Cardinal

[7] Jn 2:5.
[8] *Baltimore Catechism*, Lesson 1, answer to question no. 5.
[9] Lk 10:16.

Gonzales naming her "Queen of Quito". Corona-
tions and royal titles appeal to the Tradition-minded
because they smack of monarchy and old-school
pomp and circumstance.

The irony is that the coronation was performed
within the celebration of a *Novus Ordo* Mass according to the revised *Order of Crowning an Image of the
Blessed Virgin Mary* mandated by Pope Saint John
Paul II and published by the Congregation for
Divine Worship and the Discipline of the Sacraments in 1981.

Also in 1991, the Conceptionist convent church
was named an archdiocesan Marian sanctuary, making it an official place of pilgrimage. But this elevation
of the status of the convent church—not to mention
the cause for Mother Mariana's beatification—was
likewise performed entirely under *Novus Ordo* auspices. Now if the "post-conciliar Church" is heretical, invalid, or merely overly liberal, why should she
honor such a visionary as Mother Mariana or validate a prophetic message such as that of Our Lady
of Good Success in the first place?

It's rather like the Fundamentalist argument that
the Church kept the Bible in a dead language for
centuries so the common people wouldn't know
the truth about what's "really" in it. But, if only
churchmen had the Bible, why didn't they simply
rewrite the Scriptures to fit their alleged "false doctrines"? Obviously the Church did not suppress or
change the Bible, because she believes the Bible to

be true. She just rejects Fundamentalist interpretations of it.

Similarly, why doesn't the modern Church just ignore Mother Mariana and Our Lady of Good Success? Why give the Traditionalists more ammunition? Because the Church has judged the apparition worthy of belief. She just rejects Traditionalist interpretations of it.

Since my visit to Quito, I have undertaken to "mainstream" devotion to Mary of Good Success in the Anglophone world. Through Pro Multis Media, I produced the 2008 DVD *Our Lady of Good Success: History Miracles and Prophecies* and have subsequently written a 2012 booklet, *Mary of Good Success and the Restoration of the Church*. We also set up a website (maryofgoodsuccess.org), and I recorded a 2014 audio CD for Lighthouse Catholic Media that was chosen for their CD of the Month club: *Our Lady of Good Success Made Known for Our Time*. The point is, the message of our Lady is a profound message of hope for the whole Church, not merely the Traditionalist subculture. And the message is spreading, just as Mary said it would.

A SHOCKING DISCOVERY

Since 2007, I have spoken about Mary of Good Success at parishes, conferences, and retreats all over the United States and Canada as well as Australia and recently at a medieval monastery in Germany.

Flying home from one such talk in 2014, I was reading a newly translated abridgment of the 1790 *Life of Mother Mariana*[10] that had been sent to me by the author. I did not realize at the time that he was a priest of the SSPX. In the footnotes of the book he related an incident that had somehow managed to escape my attention—namely, that Archbishop Marcel Lefebvre invoked Our Lady of Good Success in his sermon at the infamous consecration of the four SSPX bishops in 1988. He told the story of the convent, the apparitions, the miraculous statue, and our Lady's warnings about the crisis in the twentieth century. The archbishop said:

> I excuse myself for continuing this account of the apparition, but she speaks of *a prelate who will absolutely oppose this wave of apostasy and impiety— saving the priesthood by forming good priests.* I do not say that the prophecy refers to me. You may draw your own conclusions. I was stupefied when reading these lines but I cannot deny them, since they are recorded and deposited in the archives of this apparition.[11]

I was "stupefied" to learn about the archbishop's reference, especially considering the February 2, 1634, apparition of Mary of Good Success. On

[10] Manuel Sousa Pereira, *The Admirable Life of Madre Mariana de Jesus Torres* (Los Angeles: Tradition in Action, 2005).

[11] Rev. Paul M. Kimball, trans., *The Story of Our Lady of Good Success and Novena: An Abridgement of the Book Written by Reverend Father Manuel Sousa Pereira* (Camillus, NY: Dolorosa Press, 2013), 80–81n31.

that day our Lady and the Child Jesus appeared to
Mother Mariana and, according to Father Kimball's
translation, our Lord promised His temporal pro-
tection to the Convent of the Immaculate Conception "until the end of time". He then told
Mother Mariana,

> In disastrous times I will govern [the convent]
> according to My pleasure and will, by means of My
> vicars on earth, residing in Rome, city of the popes
> of unconquered and intrepid faith. They ought to
> obey and recognize the pope as My representa-
> tive on earth, and *render him blind obedience*. He will
> be the blessed pope of My Heavenly Father and
> will reign with me in Heaven.[12]

Father Kimball attempts to mitigate this saying
of our Lord in an accompanying footnote, but I
could not fail to see the irony: the same book that
recounts how Jesus Himself made obedience to the
pope obligatory in troubled times also relates how
Marcel Lefebvre rather impiously suggested *he* was
the prelate prophesied to restore the priesthood—
during an act of *direct disobedience* to the pope!

I went to Ecuador in part hoping to validate my
Traditionalism. I came home resolved to return to
the diocesan structure. Although I strongly believed
that's what Mary wanted, I felt like I had painted myself into a corner. My family was firmly attached
to the community at Saint Incognito. In fact, it
was the only church our youngest children had

[12] Ibid., pp. 72–73.

154 CONFESSIONS OF A TRADITIONAL CATHOLIC

ever really known. Furthermore, for all my misgivings, I was also attached to the community at Saint Incognito—I didn't really *want* to leave either. Placing my confidence in God's Providence, I went ahead with the documentary and trusted our Lady would provide a solution.

I should have known I had only to look to her Son's Vicar on earth.

CHAPTER TEN

SUMMORUM PONTIFICUM AND BEYOND

When I got home from Ecuador in February 2007, I had a year's work ahead of me writing a script, taping more interviews, recording narration, and editing it all together with the footage I shot in Quito. At the same time, I was wrestling with what I perceived as the explicit desire of Our Lady of Good Success that I return my family to the formal structure of the Church—but I was not quite sure how to proceed. Little did I know, that summer the Holy Father himself would supply the answer.

The history of post-conciliar papal permissions to celebrate the Traditional Mass goes back to the 1971 "Agatha Christie Indult". This is the nickname given to Pope Paul VI's permission for celebrating the Old Mass in England and Wales. The indult was granted in response to a petition signed by several prominent Englishmen, including two Anglican bishops and the celebrated mystery writer.

In 1984, the Congregation for Divine Worship and the Discipline of the Sacraments, under Pope John Paul II, published *Quattuor abhinc annos*, granting diocesan bishops permission to allow the celebrations of Mass according to the 1962 Missal, under certain conditions, for priests and lay people who requested it. After Archbishop Lefebvre's illicit consecrations of the four SSPX bishops, Saint John Paul issued his apostolic letter *Ecclesia Dei*, given motu proprio, recommending a "wide and generous application of the directives" of the 1984 indult.[1] He also set up the Pontifical Commission *Ecclesia Dei* to care for those priests who broke from the SSPX over the illicit episcopal consecrations and to help other Traditionalist Catholics in a state of separation to return to full communion with the Church, as well as to help satisfy the just aspirations of all those Catholics who desired to assist at the Traditional Latin Mass.

On July 18, 1988, the Priestly Fraternity of Saint Peter or FSSP (Latin, *Fraternitas Sacerdotalis Sancti Petri*) was established by twelve priests and a score of seminarians formerly of the SSPX as a Catholic Society of Apostolic Life in full communion with the Holy See. Today, the FSSP constitutes the

[1] John Paul II, apostolic letter *Ecclesia Dei* (July 2, 1988), no. 6, http://www.vatican.va/roman_curia/pontifical_commissions/ecclsdei/documents/hf_jp-ii_motu-proprio_02071988_ecclesia-dei_en.html.

largest Traditional Catholic group in full communion with the Church.[2]

Then, on July 7, 2007, Benedict XVI promulgated his motu proprio *Summorum Pontificum*, generally liberating the celebration of the Traditional Latin Mass. He declared that any priest of the Roman Rite may privately celebrate Mass according to the 1962 Missal without the need of any special permission—and *publicly* with the approval of his pastor.

Although for decades many in the Church believed that the promulgation of the New Mass meant the Traditional Latin Mass was forbidden, in the letter to the bishops that accompanied *Summorum Pontificum*, the Holy Father said the Traditional Latin Mass was "never abrogated" and further:

> What earlier generations held as sacred, remains sacred and great for us too, and it cannot be all of a sudden entirely forbidden or even considered harmful.[3]

[2] The FSSP consists of 270 priests, 23 deacons, and 132 nondeacon seminarians. The FSSP clergy serve 226 Mass centers and 38 personal parishes in 124 dioceses around the world. Priestly Fraternity of Saint Peter, "What Are We? A Few Figures ...", Statistics as of October 24, 2016, https://www.fssp.org/en/chiffres.htm.

[3] Letter of His Holiness Benedict XVI to the Bishops on the Occasion of the Publication of the Apostolic Letter "Motu Proprio Data" Summorum Pontificum on the Use of the Roman Liturgy Prior to the Reform of 1970 (July 7, 2007), http://w2.vatican.va/content/benedict-xvi/en/letters/2007/documents/hf_ben-xvi_let_20070707_lettera-vescovi.html.

According to our pope emeritus there are not two rites, but two *expressions* of the one Roman Rite of Mass: the *Novus Ordo Missae* and the Traditional Latin Mass represented by the 1962 Roman Missal. Appropriately, he dubbed the New Mass the "*Forma ordinaria*" (ordinary Form) and the Traditional Mass the "*Forma extraordinaria*" (extraordinary Form).

Unfortunately, there remains widespread confusion about the legitimacy of the Extraordinary Form among "rank-and-file" Catholics, and, conversely, some Traditionalists continue to regard the Ordinary Form as illegitimate. These attitudes stem from a long-held narrative without which the Church of today is incomprehensible to many Catholics— namely, that Vatican II was a rupture with the past, a break with Tradition. For the Progressives, this "rupture" validates the introduction of various novelties unknown in the history of the Church, while, for the Traditionalists, this interpretation justifies their resistance not merely to errors or abuses, but to the new Mass itself.

HERMENEUTIC OF CONTINUITY

In the face of this double-edged sword, Benedict XVI spent his pontificate boldly declaring that the Second Vatican Council was not a break with Tradition. He called upon all Catholics to reject what he called the "hermeneutic[4] of discontinuity and

---

[4] A method or theory of interpretation.

rupture",[5] and embrace a "hermeneutic of continuity".[6] In other words, interpretations of Vatican II that are incompatible with the Church's Tradition must be corrected, while, on the other hand, it must be recognized that the documents of Vatican II can—at the very least—admit of an interpretation consistent with the Church's Tradition.[7] Applying this hermeneutic to the Mass, the pope told the bishops, "There is no contradiction between the two editions of the Roman Missal. In the history of the liturgy there is growth and progress, but no rupture," adding, "It behooves all of us to preserve the riches which have developed in the Church's faith and prayer, and to give them their proper place."[8]

This hermeneutic of continuity expressed what I had held from the beginning. That the Second Vatican Council and the New Mass represented a

[5] Address of His Holiness Benedict XVI to the Roman Curia, Offering Them His Christmas Greetings (December 22, 2005), http:// w2.vatican.va/content/benedict-xvi/en/speeches/2005/december /documents/hf_ben_xvi_spe_20051222_roman-curia.html.

[6] Benedict XVI, post-synodal apostolic exhortation *Sacramentum Caritatis* (February 22, 2007), note 6 (in note 6, Pope Benedict refers readers to his Address to the Roman Curia on December 22, 2005), http://w2.vatican.va/content/benedict-xvi/en/apost_exhortations /documents/hf_ben-xvi_exh_20070222_sacramentum-caritatis.html.

[7] In 1988 Cardinal Ratzinger conceded that not all documents of Vatican II have the same authority. Cf. Joseph Cardinal Ratzinger, Address to the Bishops of Chile (Santiago, July 13, 1988), http://unavoce .org/resources/cardinal-ratzingers-address-to-bishops-of-chile/.

[8] Letter to the Bishops on the Occasion of the Publication of the Apostolic Letter "Motu Proprio Data" Summorum Pontificum.

change in pastoral emphasis, but not in doctrine. Naturally, it's going to take time for this to sink in. Because, as the pope himself pointed out, it must be acknowledged that the changes in Catholic life and practice have caused considerable dismay among the faithful.

The "Council of the Media"

In what has been called his last "master class", Pope Benedict XVI addressed the clergy of Rome on the topic of Vatican II as he saw it. After speaking about the Council itself, its profundity and essential ideas as well as his role as a "peritus",[9] Pope Benedict brought up a final topic—what he called the "Council of the Media":

> There was the Council of the Fathers—the real Council—but there was also the Council of the media. It was almost a Council apart, and the world perceived the Council through the latter, through the media. Thus, the Council that reached the people with immediate effect was that of the media, not that of the Fathers.... The Council of journalists, naturally, was not conducted within the faith, but within the categories of today's media, namely apart from faith, with a different hermeneutic. It was a political hermeneutic: for the media, the Council was a political struggle,

[9] Expert theological advisor.

a power struggle between different trends in the Church. It was obvious that the media would take the side of those who seemed to them more closely allied with their world.[10]

He stopped short of mentioning that several prominent progressive theologians were willing contributors to this "virtual council" who lent credibility to the Council of the Media and, in the process, provided a wealth of errors and ambiguities that the Traditionalists would employ to condemn the Council of the Fathers. The soon-to-be pope emeritus said the virtual council had "no interest in liturgy as an act of faith, but as something where comprehensible things are done, a matter of community activity, something profane ... a community act, with communal participation: participation understood as activity".[11] These ideas, he said, "were virulent in the process of putting the liturgical reform into practice; they were born from a vision of the Council *detached* from its proper key, that of faith".[12]

He declared that since this Council of the media was "the more effective one" and "accessible to everyone", it "was stronger than the real Council"

[10] Address of His Holiness Pope Benedict XVI, Meeting with the Parish Priests and the Clergy of Rome (February 14, 2013), http://w2.vatican.va/content/benedict-xvi/en/speeches/2013/february/documents/hf_ben-xvi_spe_20130214_clero-roma.html.

[11] Ibid.

[12] Ibid.

and "created so many disasters, so many problems, so much suffering: seminaries closed, convents closed, banal liturgy".[13] However, he stated the real strength of the Council remained present and has slowly emerged and "became the true force which is also the true reform, the true renewal of the Church. It seems to me," he said, "that, 50 years after the Council, we see that this virtual Council is broken, is lost, and there now appears the true Council with all its spiritual force."[14] His all-too-brief pontificate is a case in point.

In particular, I cannot overemphasize the impact *Summorum Pontificum* had on me. I did not dream to see so much progress in my lifetime, much less all at once on the pope's "own initiative". Naturally, I was not in the least surprised when the Progressives accused Pope Benedict of "turning back the clock" and "betraying the Council" and so forth, nor did I expect an "about-face" on the part of the SSPX, whose issues go well beyond the Mass. But I was disappointed that the document did not cause more of a stir in my little Independent Traditionalist community. If it is really "the Mass that matters", then the motu proprio should have been an occasion for rejoicing; instead, it received a hearty round of indifference. As I feared, being "Independent" had become such a badge of identity that it simply

[13] Ibid.
[14] Ibid.

didn't matter that the pope himself was taking the initiative to restore the celebration of the Traditional Mass and Sacraments.

For our part, Pro Multis Media immediately produced an audio presentation, *What Every Catholic Needs to Know about the Traditional Mass* (2007), to help "ordinary" Catholics understand the differences between the two forms and, most importantly, to realize that they are *not* in contradiction. Unfortunately, considering the fate of Saint Anonymous, I feared that *Summorum Pontificum* would be a dead letter in my own diocese. How wonderful it was to be proven wrong.

BACK IN THE SADDLE

Not long after the publication of the motu proprio, I received a phone call from a former fellow parishioner from Saint Anonymous. She had moved to another state, but was excited about Benedict XVI's motu proprio and wanted to know if my family and I would now be assisting at the Extraordinary Form in a diocesan church. I said we would if we could, but I knew of no such opportunity. As it turns out, she had called precisely to share the news that a certain nearby diocesan church had, without fanfare, begun offering the Extraordinary Form. Ironically, the person who called to share this news was the very same who encouraged us to attend Saint Incognito in the first place.

It was the answer to a prayer. That we now had easy access to a Traditional Mass that was both valid and licit left me no choice but to return to the diocesan structure. That Sunday I "pulled the Dad card", packed us into the family van, and headed back into full communion with the local ordinary.

Our return to the embrace of the Church was just a matter of Confession, as well as some gentle "deprogramming" on the part of the two oldest children. This homecoming was the most difficult for my eldest son, who for one year had attended the school at Saint Incognito and been well and truly indoctrinated into the Traditionalist mindset. The irony of the situation was not lost on me. After all, it was precisely because I promised to raise my children in the Catholic faith that Macklin's question about the Eucharist all those years ago had prompted me to take RCIA. A journey began for our family with that simple question that radically affected us all. Thanks be to God and the intercession of the Blessed Virgin Mary, that journey had now come full circle.

THE OLD MASS AND THE
NEW EVANGELIZATION

Seven years later, I visited Australia. It started with an invitation to give the keynote address at an annual fundraising dinner, but, before I knew it, I had agreed to give nine presentations over the course of seven days at various locations in Brisbane, Sydney, and Melbourne, including a cathedral, a Catholic college, a live radio broadcast, and several parish churches.

During this memorable week, I had the pleasure of speaking at both Latin and Eastern Rite communities. It was a powerful and humbling reminder that the Mass is a reality that transcends the "rite"; otherwise, we would not have so many valid liturgical traditions in the Church. It is well for Traditionalists to remember that the Missal of Pius V was never imposed on the Eastern Rites of the Church, or even on Latin Rites more than two hundred years old. The truth is, the one Paschal Mystery of Christ has always been celebrated by the Church according to a multitude of rites because

> the unfathomable richness of the mystery of Christ cannot be exhausted by any single liturgical tradition. From the very beginning, therefore, this richness found expression among various peoples and cultures in ways that are characterized by a wonderful diversity and complementarity.[15]

By what criterion does the Church assure unity in the midst of this plurality?

---

[15] *Compendium of the Catechism of the Catholic Church*, no. 247 (cf. CCC 1200–1204; 1207–9).

It is fidelity to the Apostolic Tradition, that is, the communion in the faith and in the sacraments received from the apostles, a communion that is both signified and guaranteed by apostolic succession.[16]

Remember, the apostolic succession was the intellectual lynchpin of my conversion. It is precisely because the Church is Catholic and apostolic that she can integrate into her unity the authentic riches of all the various rites. It seems to me, if the Church can embrace twenty-three Eastern liturgical rites, surely she can support *two* expressions of the *one* Roman Rite.

One of the highlights of my visit "down under" was spending some "quality time" with the priests of the Brisbane Oratory in Formation. They are attached to a local parish where they celebrate both forms of the Mass that are served by young men from the local Frassati group.[17] The reverence of both clergy and laity were every bit as inspiring at their Ordinary Form Mass as at their Extraordinary Form Mass. When I complimented them on their liturgy and community, one of the young men asked if I considered them unique, or if I had encountered similar situations in North America. I replied that I had, and, in fact, many times. But I could not say whether it was a general trend, or if

[16] Ibid., no. 248 (cf. *CCC* 1209).
[17] A young-adult organization dedicated to the lay spirituality of Blessed Pier Giorgio Frassati, T.O.S.D.

it was only typical of the type of parish that would invite me to speak!

COMMON GROUND

The point is, I *have* travelled throughout the continental United States and Canada and, increasingly, outside North America. In the process I have encountered some common traits in those parishes that celebrate both forms of the Mass. They tend to have a lot of lay involvement, Eucharistic Adoration (often perpetual), long lines for Confession, a refreshingly reverent celebration of the New Mass, and a genuine sense of community.

Like most human endeavors, there is usually a core group that does the lion's share of the work, and these communities are no different. But my experience suggests that when lay people are willing to demonstrate their desire for a more reverent liturgy, and the clergy are responsive, there follows a positive reaction from the community at large. I think the fact that the initiative comes "from below" is key. Most people don't like change in the first place and *really* don't like to have it imposed upon them from above. But when ordinary parishioners spontaneously initiate a return to reverence, it tends to be contagious. Why? First, I think that many Catholics secretly long for it, and second, I believe it strikes a chord even in those who "don't know what they're missing". It is the only explanation I can give to the significant number of mainstream Catholic bloggers who made a hero of Benedict XVI for his celebration of the Ordinary Form. Catholics who would never dream of assisting at a Traditional Mass were naturally drawn to his liturgical "style". Of course, his secret was that he had no "style" at all. He simply and reverently followed the rubrics with the docility of a celebrant who knows the Mass is not about him—*or the people*—but about all of us worshipping the Father, through the Son, in the Holy Spirit.

In contrast, I recently attended Mass at a parish where the priest was determined to get the folks "fired up" by continually prompting nonliturgical responses and applause. It was clear that most people were uncomfortable and that the poor priest was utterly clueless. Apparently, according to his formation, a "successful" liturgy must resemble a popular entertainment. But the Catholic *sensus fidei* naturally rebels against treating the liturgy like a show, hence the lackluster response. In my humble opinion, this may also explain the exodus from the Church on the part of some young adult Catholics who have attended years of liturgy chock-full of profane elements in a largely fruitless attempt to make Mass "more relevant". The fact is, the world can do entertainment better than your youth Mass ever can—a lot better—but only the Mass gives us the opportunity to participate with all the angels and saints in the heavenly liturgy; the Holy Mass alone is heaven on earth. This is where the emphasis *must* be regardless of the form being celebrated.

I have seen the evidence with my own eyes, again and again. The impressive depth of the informal conversation among the young adult men and women of the Frassati group in Brisbane powerfully demonstrated to me that their formation included much more than pep talks and pop songs. Surely there is a place for both in the lives of young people, but it need not be at Holy Mass.

MUTUALLY ENRICHING

In the letter to the bishops that accompanied *Summorum Pontificum*, Benedict XVI made it clear that "the new Missal will certainly remain the ordinary Form of the Roman Rite, not only on account of the juridical norms, but also because of the actual situation of the communities of the faithful."[18] For one thing, he said, "use of the old Missal presupposes a certain degree of liturgical formation" and "knowledge of the Latin language"[19] that many priests simply do not possess today.

He also offered his personal witness that the Traditional Movement began "above all because in many places celebrations were not faithful to

---

[18] Letter to the Bishops on the Occasion of the Publication of the Apostolic Letter "Motu Proprio Data" Summorum Pontificum.

[19] Ibid.

the prescriptions of the new Missal, but [it] actually was understood as *authorizing or even requiring creativity*, which frequently led to *deformations of the liturgy* which were hard to bear."[20] And, I dare say, *remain* hard to bear. This liturgical poverty remains the number-one complaint I hear from the faithful all over North America. Even in the many parishes where there is no specific desire for the Traditional liturgy, there is still a deep longing for reverence and sacrality that all too often goes needlessly unfulfilled.

The pope emeritus expressed his conviction that "the two Forms of the usage of the Roman Rite can be mutually enriching" and that the celebration of the New Mass has the potential to "demonstrate, *more powerfully than has been the case hitherto*, the sacrality which attracts many people to the former usage".[21] He said:

> The most sure guarantee that the Missal of Paul VI can unite parish communities and be loved by them consists in its being celebrated with great reverence in harmony with the liturgical directives. This will bring out the spiritual richness and the theological depth of this Missal.[22]

In my travels, I have discovered this "reverence in harmony with the liturgical directives" more

[20] Ibid.
[21] Ibid.
[22] Ibid.

often on display at those parishes where both forms of the Roman Rite are celebrated.

WHAT'S A FATHER TO DO?

We have demonstrated that the post-conciliar popes from Paul VI to Benedict XVI have taught that there is no rupture between the old and new forms of the Mass. However, Benedict XVI especially recognized what I call a "rupture of experience". The truth is many of today's faithful are profoundly estranged from the devotional atmosphere common to their ancestors.

A big step toward a return to the vision of the Council of the Fathers was the 2010 publication of the New English Translation of the Roman Missal.[23] This new translation is more accurate and faithful to the Latin text, as well as more respectful of its structure and substance. It has been rendered all the richer through the use of formal language that better preserves the traditional character and style of the Roman Rite. Along with this new translation, there are a number of concrete steps individual priests can take to begin to heal the "rupture of experience". Choosing from the available options those most consonant with Tradition is one

---

[23] This 2010 translation of the Missal of Paul VI by the International Committee on English in the Liturgy (ICEL) is the fruit of the 2001 instruction *Liturgiam Authenticam*.

simple way the celebrant can enrich the Ordinary Form right away. Professor of theology Peter Kwasniewski refers to this as the "continuity principle".[24]

Among others, he suggests the following sample choices: Father may read or chant the entrance and Communion antiphons; choose Penitential Rite A (which includes the Confiteor and the Kyrie); make use of the conventional translation "brethren" rather than the optional "brothers and sisters" at invitations to prayer and encourage lay lectors to do the same at the beginning of readings; pray the Roman Canon (Eucharistic Prayer I) in its entirety, complete with the litany of saints; hold his thumb and forefingers together from the Consecration until the ablutions; use incense whenever appropriate; bow noticeably over the host and chalice while reciting the words of Consecration slowly and deliberately; omit the invitation to share the "sign of peace" (which is optional); perform the ablutions thoroughly in the traditional manner using wine, then water, then wine; bow his head at the name of the three divine Persons named together and at the name of Jesus, Mary, and the saint of the day, instructing servers and readers to do the same.[25]

---

[24] Peter Kwasniewski, "Imbuing the Ordinary Form with Extraordinary Form Spirituality", New Liturgical Movement, April 13, 2015, http://www.newliturgicalmovement.org/2015/04/imbuing-ordinary -form-with.html#.WWBqZeRvS3A.

[25] Ibid. (The instruction regarding the bowing of the head can be found in GIRM 234.)

As Dr. Kwasniewski points out, these options are all permitted by the *Novus Ordo* rubrics and depend primarily on the priest. With the exception of the use of incense and the traditional ablutions, which require some training of servers, none of these suggestions entail any special preparation or expense.

But what about the Extraordinary Form? How is the Traditional liturgy enriched by the New Mass? In my opinion, the answer lies in two words: *active participation*. For a hundred years, the popes encouraged the faithful to follow the prayers of the Missal and to learn, in Latin, the prayers and responses proper to the congregation. That the faithful as a rule remained in their "usual torpor", as Paul VI would have it, is what led to the New Order of the Mass in the first place.

But after decades of the new liturgy, "active participation" is well and truly ingrained in the Catholic consciousness. At the Extraordinary Form Mass we attend weekly, most people either bring their own Missals or follow along with Latin/English or Latin/Spanish "Missalettes" provided by the parish. We enjoy the efforts of an excellent choir and schola, and many in the congregation join in chanting the Latin prayers and responses. Another parish in our diocese celebrates a Sunday Extraordinary Form wherein the Introit, Collects, and Bible readings are all done in the vernacular as allowed by *Summorum Pontificum*, and I have encountered the same situation in other dioceses as well. I suspect that the typical celebration of the Extraordinary Form under diocesan auspices today is very much what was envisioned by Pope Saint Pius X and largely fulfils the prescriptions of the Vatican II Constitution on the Sacred Liturgy.

Of course there is room for further mutual enrichment. In *Summorum Pontificum*, Pope Benedict suggested that the prefaces and prayers for new saint days can and should be integrated in the Extraordinary Form, while Cardinal Sarah, the current Prefect of the Congregation for Divine Worship and the Discipline of the Sacraments, recently suggested that the traditional Offertory prayers be restored to the Ordinary Form as well as advocating a return to celebrating *ad orientum*.[26] In any case, it has become clear to me that we must move beyond internecine bickering and embrace the truth that our worship of God goes beyond the rite in which it is celebrated.

The Latin liturgy concludes with the words *Ite, Missa est*, "Go forth, the Mass is ended." This ending, then, is also a beginning. We are "sent forth" into the world "to love and serve the Lord" so that our worship may continue in a multitude of ways. As Scripture shows, worship is a way of life in which we offer our bodies and minds as living sacrifices.[27]

[26] Robert Cardinal Sarah, "The Silent Action of the Heart", Adoremus.org, July 15, 2015. The original text appeared in Italian with the title "*Silenziosa azione del cuore*", in *L'Osservatore Romano*, June 12, 2015; translation by Christopher Ruff, https://adoremus .org/2015/07/15/silent-action-heart/.

[27] Rom 12:1–2.

We honor God when we evangelize,[28] when we support apostolic work,[29] and when we help others,[30] just to name a few examples. In all these ways and more we worship God "in spirit and truth".[31]

I write these words with an appreciation of how blessed I am to be in full communion with the Church as I live out my primary vocation of husband and father. I am privileged to attend the Extraordinary Form Mass on Sundays and Holy Days of Obligation with my family and to teach RCIA with the blessing of the diocese. I speak regularly at parishes and Catholic conferences and have the honor to work with such apostolates as Lighthouse Catholic Media, Augustine Institute, Saint Joseph Communications, Ignatius Press, and, of course, Pro Multis Media. While I still consider myself a Traditional Catholic, I do not scruple to assist at the Ordinary Form, especially on weekdays and when travelling domestically and internationally to promote devotion to the Blessed Virgin Mary, Mother of the Church.

A FINAL WORD

Not long after my conversion, Betty told me she had been praying for me since she was a little girl. I replied, "That's a good trick considering we met in

[28] Rom 15:16.
[29] Phil 4:18.
[30] Heb 13:16.
[31] Jn 4:24.

our twenties!" She explained, "When I was seven years old I discerned I did not have a vocation to the religious life. I figured that meant I would be a wife and mother, so I started praying for the man I would marry someday." Looking back over my former life with the eyes of faith, I can see the many graces I was granted through her daily Hail Mary's. Because, while Betty didn't know who she was going to marry someday, God certainly did.

So our Lady was interceding for me decades before it ever entered into my mind or heart to become a Catholic. And she's been there for me ever since. Even when I left the diocesan structure, she was there for me, pointing the way back, interceding with her Divine Son to bring good results out of my less than perfect choices. She is there for me still. She is there for all of us.

The Church today faces many challenges, but Mary promised her "Good Success" at a time to come "when almost all will seem lost and paralyzed", so I suspect things may get worse before they get better. But I also believe that the promised restoration of the Church is already under way, and that the mutual enrichment of the two forms of the Roman Rite is a visible sign of that restoration. I am further convinced—if God's way of Fathering his Chosen People in the Old Testament is any indication—that things will continue to improve in direct proportion to our fidelity to the Church and her official liturgy in whatever form or rite.